STITCHING THE
24-HOUR CITY

STITCHING THE 24-HOUR CITY

Life, Labor, and the Problem
of Speed in Seoul

Seo Young Park

CORNELL UNIVERSITY PRESS   ITHACA AND LONDON

First published 2021 by Cornell University Press

Library of Congress Cataloging-in-Publication Data

Names: Park, Seo Young, 1979- author.
Title: Stitching the 24-hour city : life, labor, and the problem of speed in Seoul / Seo Young Park.
Description: Ithaca [New York] : Cornell University Press, 2021. | Includes bibliographical references and index.
Identifiers: LCCN 2020043492 (print) | LCCN 2020043493 (ebook) | ISBN 9781501754265 (hardcover) | ISBN 9781501756115 (paperback) | ISBN 9781501754272 (pdf) | ISBN 9781501754289 (epub)
Subjects: LCSH: Clothing workers—Korea (South)—Seoul—Social life and customs—21st century. | Ready-to-wear clothing industry—Korea (South)—Seoul. | Markets—Social aspects—Korea (South)—Seoul. | Social ecology—Korea (South)—Seoul. | Tongdaemun-gu (Seoul, Korea)—Social conditions—21st century.
Classification: LCC HD8039.C62 K67 2021 (print) | LCC HD8039.C62 (ebook) | DDC 305.9/688095195—dc23
LC record available at https://lccn.loc.gov/2020043492
LC ebook record available at https://lccn.loc.gov/2020043493

Contents

STITCHING THE
24-HOUR CITY

PROLOGUE

Oksun[1] was sitting in front of a sewing machine, carefully stitching a woman's jacket. It was a fashionable design that fused Korean traditional fabric patterns with a Western-style silhouette and was to be used as a sample for students to replicate in an advanced sewing class that Oksun was teaching at a nonprofit organization, MANI.[2] MANI's mission was to encourage slow-paced, artisanal approaches to garment production and ultimately help garment workers in Dongdaemun[3] market to achieve better working conditions for their labor.

Oksun was fifty-six years old. It was forty years ago when she had begun her work in Dongdaemun in the heart of Seoul. Since then, she had seen Dongdaemun go through many transformations and become a high-speed, fast-fashion marketplace. The political motivations behind MANI's work were not new, as Dongdaemun market had a long history of labor activism extending back many years to when high-speed mass manufacturing first became a hallmark of its production. Once a symbol of manual labor and labor struggles from the 1960s and 1980s, the market's speedy production, in which each garment only requires roughly two days to evolve from concept to finished product, has turned Dongdaemun into a transnationally popular urban cluster of garment factories, wholesalers, and retail malls. Its ceaseless pace of productivity, which extends well into the night, makes Dongdaemun one of Seoul's most potent symbols of the 24-hour city.

The class that Oksun was teaching was directed at seamstresses who were accustomed to working with machines. The class was intended to help them develop more sophisticated, intricate hand-stitching techniques and learn to *slow down* their work. MANI also envisioned a market in which garment workers would be able to engage in the production of clothes at a slower pace, giving care and attention to each piece they made, ultimately transforming themselves from "laborers" into "artisans."

As Oksun worked on the garment sample, I sat next to her, watched her, and asked her questions about her life and work. This was a typical scene from my years of studying and interviewing people in Dongdaemun market, people who were often too busy with their work to meet me at any other time. Oksun's daily life consisted of moving frequently between different factories: during the day she went to her regular job at a stitching factory, and three times a week in the evening, she came to teach MANI's workshop.

As Oksun embodied these multiple paces of work, like those whom I met in Dongdaemun, she articulated the meaning of her work within her life. I wondered how garment workers like Oksun made sense of the conflicting physical and emotional demands of work and self in an industry that creates commodities at such a quick pace. Oksun and her peers work in an industry that has often been criticized for its dehumanizing work conditions, such as long hours and physically demanding labor; yet these women live, love, grow, create, and persist here despite these circumstances. How then, I wondered, do women like Oksun understand their lives and their labor within the various frameworks of their work?

Oksun described to me how she found confidence when she was sewing on her machine. When applying for new jobs, for example, she might feel nervous, but when she was able to sit down at the sewing machine, she could begin working completely comfortably and of her own accord.

"Sitting at the machine," she said,

> whatever kind the clothes are, I feel comfortable and confident when my fingers move the fabric pieces without hesitation, making the stitches even and smooth. Speed is very important for making even stitches. If you hesitate, slow down, or pause to figure out how to do it right, you do not get smooth lines. . . . This flow determines the final fit and line of the product. You must not lose it. . . . That [flow] is a *moment of pure concentration*. . . . This is what I do and what I do well.[4]

It is clear that Oksun sees both the skills that she has built up over her long career and a sense of herself in the description of this "moment of pure concentration" when she is at the sewing machine. There she feels attuned to the rhythms and pace of her fingertips and feels connected to her own work. Although there is no certificate program or use of résumés to formally account for a seamstress's career and talents, Oksun proves herself to be a skilled worker in other ways. Through quick and competent sewing work, Oksun demonstrates to potential employers that she is a desirable and flexible worker for the just-in-time labor that characterizes Dongdaemun market. Yet, at the same time, this fast-paced workflow also includes moments when the smooth orchestration of her body, the material, and the machine reveals Oksun's keen sense of self and intimate attachment to her work. This perspective—where Oksun meaningfully engages with her work—is neither part of the dominant critiques of labor exploitation that define garment workers as an alienated part of the manufacturing machine nor part of the narrative promoted by the South Korean state that presents garment workers as now-vanishing and replaceable figures of the past.

Sitting at the sewing machine, workers like Oksun create a sense of attachment to their labor through the flow of their work, amid these moments of embodied and affective attunement to the various tempos of labor and life. The multiple tempos consist of the cycles of commodity production and circulation, the recurrent construction and destruction of built environments, and the shifting days and nights, cycles of payments and transactions, and the rhythms of lives shared with family and friends. This ethnography unfolds stories that show how this kind of flow both enables and counters the dominant "speed" of garment production and circulation that is vital to the market. How does Oksun's own flow interact with the paces of other actors in the market and in the city? How does the flow of Oksun's sewing, where she finds a sense of attachment to her work and her own vitality as a worker and member of the market, respond to the critiques of speed prevalent in the labor and urban politics of South Korea? In the conclusion, the book will revisit this opening vignette concerning Oksun.

INTRODUCTION

"Our work? It's like *quick service*," Jiyoung, an experienced clothing designer, said to me as I shadowed her during a workday in Dongdaemun market. *Kuikseobiseu*, or "quick service,"[1] is a term that is typically used for the motorbike delivery couriers that deliver small packages to anywhere in Seoul in forty to sixty minutes. Jiyoung, however, was referring to how she and many other designers in Dongdaemun can develop a garment from concept design to a ready-made item of clothing on the shelves of retail malls in two days or less. This pace of production—both for the quick-service riders and the garment designers, manufacturers, and retailers—can be seen throughout Dongdaemun market and its many outsourcing factories spread out across the narrow, hilly streets of the adjacent neighborhoods. This local marketplace, now famous for its on-demand, just-in-time production and distribution, has played a large part in the accelerated transnational fast-fashion industry that has developed across East Asia.

During my research for this book, I regularly shadowed workers in Dongdaemun market, like Jiyoung, and was able to see how the fast pace among them manifests itself as an embodied, immanent, and affective experience. This ethnography focuses on such everyday lives and the subjective narratives of those individuals. Their work sustains the fast-paced material production and distribution that defines the market, ultimately showing how these narratives shape the politics and counterpolitics of labor and the urban city.

On the day when she described her work to me as "quick service," Jiyoung was in the middle of coordinating not only the design of a new garment but its manufacture as well. The garment would later be sold in the wholesale store that she worked for.

FIGURE I.1. Quick-service motorbike. The rack is individually customized to carry heavy-duty textile rolls and garment packages.

Photo by the author.

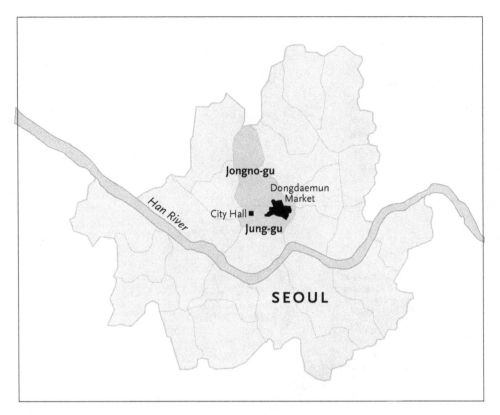

MAP I.1. The location of Dongdaemun

Courtesy of Lohnes+Wright.

I had met Jiyoung at 9:00 a.m. that morning in front of the wholesale mall apM, one of the fourteen different malls clustered around the eastern part of Dongda-emun. The multistory, modern-looking buildings are covered with glaring, colorful neon lights at night. The inside looks like an indoor marketplace, filled with count-less stalls stacked tightly against each other. By the time I arrived, Jiyoung and her design partner had already finished a brief meeting with their colleagues. Many of them had red, puffy eyes that revealed their exhaustion from having worked *all night* at their wholesale storefront.

Dongdaemun's garment manufacturing, wholesaling, and retail outlets spread across a sprawling marketplace that takes up around ten city blocks. Walking and occasionally hopping on a city bus, we followed the manufacturing cycles of two women's clothing items—a newly designed vest and a jacket (a continuing item). Under the morning sun, I followed Jiyoung and her partner to Doota, one of the

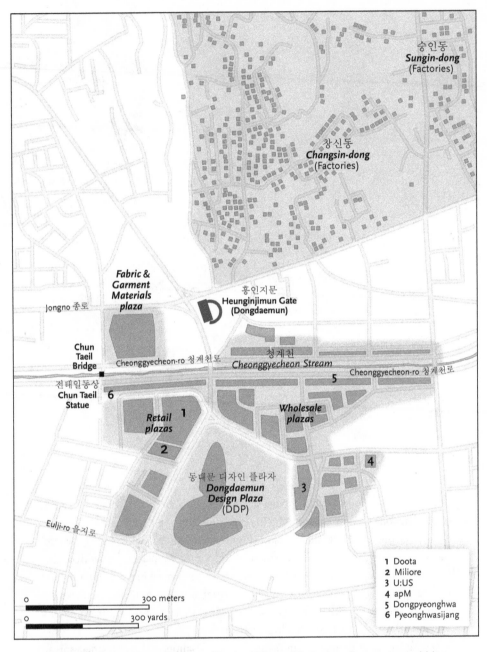

숭인동
Sungin-dong
(Factories)

창신동
Changsin-dong
(Factories)

Fabric & Garment Materials plaza

Jongno 종로

홍인지문
Heunginjimun Gate
(Dongdaemun)

Chun Taeil Bridge

Cheonggyecheon-ro 청계천로

청계천
Cheonggyecheon Stream

Cheonggyecheon-ro 청계천로

5

전태일동상
Chun Taeil Statue

6

Retail plazas

1

2

Wholesale plazas

4

동대문 디자인 플라자
Dongdaemun Design Plaza
(DDP)

3

Eulji-ro 을지로

0   300 meters
0   300 yards

1 Doota
2 Miliore
3 U:US
4 apM
5 Dongpyeonghwa
6 Pyeonghwasijang

MAP I.2. Map of Dongdaemun. The locations of factories show a general idea of where and how they are clustered and dispersed. For more exact locations, please see Seoul History Archives (2011, 99).

Courtesy of Lohnes+Wright.

seven retail shopping plazas that resemble the wholesale mall buildings we had just left. The interiors of these retail plazas differ from the wholesale venues, however, in that the six- and seven-story buildings were packed with thousands of individual retail shops and other retail facilities, such as 24-hour movie theaters, coffee shops, and saunas. After pausing to scan window displays, I noticed that the designers were increasing the pace of our walk to Dongdaemun Jonghapsijang, a big plaza filled with small-scale wholesale stores selling garment fabrics and materials. Once we arrived, Jiyoung ordered fabric, buttons, zippers, and other necessary materials for the vest she was designing. She also had more materials immediately delivered to the manufacturing factories for the jackets to be produced during the day. We made multiple rounds through the wholesale stores and then moved on to small-scale outsourcing factories in the adjacent neighborhoods of Changsin-dong, Bomun-dong, and Jang-an-dong. The designers made phone calls and visited factories all day until we returned to the wholesale market to start the night's work. As we walked through the factories, people were busy at work, expertly using the tools in their hands, such as needles and thread, scissors, patterns, fabric pieces, sewing machines, buttonhole-making machines, embroidery machines, dyeing substances, and steamer irons.

Beginning at 11:00 p.m., Dongdaemun market springs to life—the traffic gets congested, the streets fill with people, and loud music creates an energy and ambiance. All the while, packages of newly finished clothes pile up high in each storefront. We confirmed that the jackets that Jiyoung and her colleague had ordered in the morning were arriving on the sales floor from the manufacturing factories. A total of 1,200 units in various sizes and colors had been made that day. The sample vest that Jiyoung had designed earlier in the day (and had had a head seamstress at the stitching factory make) had also arrived. She made a few changes to her design and then sent the revised design to the factory again through a quick-service courier. The following morning, she approved the revised sample and sent this new design into immediate production, ordering 100 pieces in two colors and three sizes to be manufactured and delivered the next day. The vest only lasted two days on the design-to-sale track.

To move through Dongdaemun market is to duck and weave through masses of people. We navigated a space occupied by bodies strolling, walking, running, and carrying packages. The quick-service motorbikes brought deliveries from the narrow, hilly streets of the adjacent neighborhoods that housed the manufacturing units. Jiyoung aggressively cut through a group of Chinese tourists, whose slow and distracted movement created congestion in the middle of an alley. I tried my best not to get left behind, but I was now being especially cautious, as I had already twice been bumped by the gigantic fabric rolls piled on the back of motorbikes for delivery. I had grown up in Seoul and Dongdaemun was familiar to me. Yet I often felt *out of pace* following these people's work and stumbled over the differently paced movements of the bodies.

The mixed paces also extend to the landscape change. Under nearly neverending construction, like many other parts of other East Asian megacities, Dongdaemun is a dense cluster of old and new structures. The buildings vary in form and style, from low and long box-shaped warehouses, painted in fading 1970s color schemes, to futuristic plaza buildings with curvy facades made of sleek silver metal plates. These variations trace the changing functions and aesthetics of the city's industry. During my preliminary and extended fieldwork, the historic Dongdaemun Baseball Stadium built in 1925 was deconstructed, leaving a gigantic open space for several years. Toward the end of my fieldwork, the space was occupied by the swiftly constructed Dongdaemun Design Plaza—a huge, streamlined building complex, whose physical design symbolized the "flow of people" in the market. Yet the unusual shape of the structure itself intruded on the flow of working people and their movements.

The constant construction in the marketplace even included the restoration of a natural stream. Dongdaemun is bisected by Cheonggyecheon stream, which had been paved over from 1968 through 2003 and then uncovered and restored in 2005. While the resuscitated flowing stream was widely promoted as signaling the new "green" future of Seoul, when my interlocutors and I crossed this waterway multiple times throughout any given day, we often joked about its funky smell and traded rumors about the ambiguous quality of its water. While rushing to our destination, we would glance at the stream from the small bridges that spanned it and at the people strolling along the narrow banks, enjoying the "nature": bushes, rocks, water, and fish. We would only indulge in the distraction and enjoy a chat for a moment, without slowing down my interlocutors' workflow.

Jiyoung's work indeed was like a quick service, in the sense that it was swiftly moving, keeping the material object in the circuit of just-in-time production. The analogy of quick service certainly didn't leave Jiyoung feeling proud. The high-speed production and circulation overshadowed the marketplace as a problem for the general public, planners, labor activists, and workers themselves. However, her movement was not through a flat and empty space. As I navigated the space with Jiyoung and my interlocutors, the marketplace emerged as a charged space with bodies, objects, built forms, and nature, all of which were differently paced and constituted in time in disparate ways. This ethnography traces the stories of those whose work composes the temporal fabric of the marketplace, while sustaining and challenging the problem of speed—and, in doing so, reveals the tangled paces and temporality of the labor and the city.

Stitching and the Problem of Speed

Stitching 24-Hour City explores the problem of speed in its multiple forms implicated in the experiences and politics of labor, focusing on the work of garment seamstresses and designers and their presence in the city. To materialize sped-up production, workers like Oksun (introduced in the prologue) and Jiyoung spend tremendous amounts of time laboring with back-breaking intensity. In doing so, their work also induces more encounters and interactions in this particular marketplace and creates moments of concentration, attunements, and exhilaration. The intensity and complexity of sped-up work ultimately sustains the operation and fabricates the spectacle of the 24-hour city of Seoul.

The stories of work in this ethnography reveal two different relations labor has with speed for commodity production. First, increasing the speed of the production-and-circulation cycle is the primary means for increasing accumulation. As numerous labor critiques have theorized, the pressure of speed, especially in the ready-made clothes market, dictates and estranges the labor relationship workers have with the product, other labors, or their own labor itself. It also mobilizes people into a systematic hierarchy dividing them up into those who define, command, or follow the speed. Second, however, the speed is also experienced through the specificities of life and labor of the workers as they move across and dwell in the marketplace. The expedition mobilizes and mediates certain kinds of affect, intimacy, or attachment that saturate and complicate labor relations, as the workers themselves experience and make sense of their own work and their surroundings.

While these relations coexist, this first register of speed and its exploitative pressure on labor is predominant such that the near-experience temporality of labor becomes often invisible and unthinkable. Yet in reality, it is the workers themselves who *embody and stitch together* the pressure of the sped-up production process and the affective and intimate relationships formed around their fast-paced work. The book's focus on these workers' practices and narratives is not meant to ignore the structural problems and the political economy of labor. Rather, by giving an attentive look into the practice of stitching, the ethnography endeavors to understand the meanings and motivations that people find in their work despite and against the existing problems of speed that are widely known and shared.

Stitching, the basic and fine act of connecting two separate edges to fabricate a bigger piece, literally and metaphorically addresses an ethnographic lens through which we can see the contradictions of these relations. The machine stitch, the basis of ready-made garment production, involves two or three threads that are interlocked or overlocked to make even seams. The connection is tight but visible, traceable, and unlockable. The book delves into this kind of connection of interwoven loops, between the seemingly one straight line of abstract speed that urges us to see the issue of structural pressures on labor and the other thread of the speed of experience that encourages us to see the embodied and affective aspects of the work and its narrative. "A stitch at a time" in Korean, *han ttam han ttam,* usually expresses the great deal of care, time, and high-quality skill that handmade artisan clothes require, in contrast to the flattened lines of mass production. The present ethnography invites us to see that machine stitches—standing in for the labor required to design, assemble, pack, and sell ready-made fast-fashion clothing—could also carry a kind of care, passion, or attachment to one's own work. While radically different from the artisanal process of constructing by hand, fast-fashion manufacturing may still be a site where we can see individual and social narratives of labor and conceptualize the temporalities of work. These aspects of sped-up work, as the first part of the book explores, inspire others to be active at night, to sustain and amplify intimate networks, and give rise to new articulations between imitative work and creative work. To account for this, one needs to engage in-depth with microscopic practices and to possess ethnographical sensitivity toward the narratives of people who talk about their attachment.

This ethnography also addresses how speed has become a social problem in the context of South Korea. "Quick service"—Jiyoung's remark on the pressure of quick-paced work resonated incessantly throughout my interviews with other interlocutors whom I encountered in the factories and marketplace. These workers, to varying degrees, criticized the pressure that was required to keep up with the pace of production and consumption and its brutal impact on laboring bodies. The second part of the book explores how *the problematization* of speed itself has become a conduit for environmentally friendly urban projects and the development of alternative markets, like those undertaken by MANI, the organization where Oksun was working.

The long-standing historical contestation over labor and production speed, both in the South Korean political economy and within the global fashion industry, has manifested in different frames over time in Dongdaemun. While the pursuit of fast production and growth has produced the problem of labor exploitation and the top-down economic planning of the authoritarian state, it was most strongly derided as the culprit for the lack of "creativity" in the industry and Dongdaemun's notoriety for non-brand and imitation products. Over the past decade, Korean economic and urban planning commissions used the catchphrase "creative economy," "creative city," *or* "design" in their political rhetoric and construction projects to encourage the advancement of high value-added cultural and knowledge production. Dongdaemun Design Plaza and the Cheonggyecheon restoration project reflect and spatialize the idea of alternative paces of the city in the urban spectacle, rebranding and refashioning Seoul as a global, creative, and eco-friendly metropolitan center. MANI, introduced in the prologue, also saw fast-paced production as a labor problem. Founded in 2003 for local garment workers, the organization inherited the philosophy of the garment labor unions working in Dongdaemun from the 1960s to the 1980s. Like the unions, MANI problematized the persistent poor quality of garment workers' work and lives due to their arduous schedules and the demand to produce clothes twenty-four hours a day in Dongdaemun.

Though based on different kinds of problematics, both the South Korean government's and MANI's projects represent a widely spread cultural script about "speed" as a problem that workers and nonworkers both make references to and respond to in making sense of and narrating their work in Dongdaemun. At the same time, they also generate urban and labor projects invested in the future of Dongdaemun and the South Korean urban economy in general. While motivated by radically different political interests and modes of change, creating a new tempo has been the goal underlying both projects. Ironically, it is through these projects that disparate paces and logics that are embedded in the very bodies—of the laborers and the city space—become apparent. The dissident paces paradoxically persist and fabricate the current temporality—the particular sense of time—of the city and marketplace. The book shows how these practices slow down the pace of the market and the city, revealing more complexities within, and proving that the critique resides in and on the border of the very speed it has endeavored to criticize.

Fast Fashion in Place

Many features of Dongdaemun reflect the so-called fast-fashion industry that intensifies the acceleration of accumulation of goods through a flexible mode of production. As evidenced by Jiyoung's daily travels around the market and as I discuss below, the just-in-time production promotes variety in design and small batches involving intricate spatial relocations and transnational connections that evolve over time. While these features are not unique for flexible production on a global scale (Piore and Sable 1984),[2] Dongdaemun's flexibility is situated in and shapes the particular urban industrialization of Seoul and the 24-hourization of the city.

Dongdaemun began as a marketplace in the Joseon period in the early twentieth century and was formed at the north gate of Hanyang (Seoul's old name).[3] This gate, officially named Heunginjimun, was also often called Dongdaemun ("East Grand Gate") and known as the entrance to Seoul used by the lower classes and the poor. After the Korean War (1950–1953), the traditional open marketplace formed around the east gate evolved into a modern commercial space, where individual merchants gathered around its public squares, streets, and major transportation hubs. In the contemporary context, the effect can still be noted in that modern buildings and shopping plazas in Dongdaemun are called "marketplace" (*sijang*).[4]

During the heyday of mass production from the 1960s to the 1980s, Dongdaemun's buildings were filled with factories on the upper floors and wholesale shops on the ground level. The authoritarian government implemented an export-centered economic developmental plan based on low grain prices and low-wage labor and included labor-intensive garment manufacturing as one of the central industrial sectors. This broad economic plan brought a large number of underemployed rural people into the city for jobs. Dongdaemun market provided mass manufactured clothes to a growing domestic ready-made clothing market, as well as foreign apparel corporations. In this context, female workers were mobilized as cheap labor within the gendered, patriotic narrative that identified them as "industrial warriors."[5] Multiple demands were made on women's bodies while their work and workplaces were marginalized (Bonacich 1994; Lessinger 2002; Mills 2003).[6]

Seeking lower labor costs, mass-scale outsourcing factories (both Korean and foreign apparel companies) began to move to different locations in Korea and such other countries as China and Vietnam starting in late 1980s, which led many people to believe that garment production had disappeared from Seoul (Kang 1995; Mitter and Rowbotham 2003). By the 1990s, the focus of the South Korean economy shifted toward the rising consumer capitalism. However, the Asian financial crisis in 1997 and the subsequent International Monetary Fund bailout of South Korea brought about an unexpected revitalization of Dongdaemun through the exponential growth of flexible production. An increase in the domestic need for cheap clothes paralleled the growth of tourism, particularly from adjacent Japan and China (favoring the devaluation of the Korean won), highlighting the role of Dongdaemun as a retail site and place of consumption. In the first years of the 2000s, the successes of online retail in Korea sparked a trend in start-up entrepreneurship among South Korean youth—which will be detailed in later chapters and which also contributed to the continued prominence of Dongdaemun in the heart of Seoul.

Scholars and the media continue to see Dongdaemun's modern retail sector and its endless supply of designs as a new, compact model of "flexible production," with fast-paced production as the lifeblood of mass production. Today's on-the-spot process of design and production enables wholesalers to readily respond to the preferences of their buyers, whom they observe in Dongdaemun's marketplace. Relying on the proximity to the manufacturing factories, Dongdaemun's wholesalers monitor customer purchases and then respond by ordering more products to be put on display that very same night. Since a garment can be designed, produced, and put on the shelf in less than two days, this quick pace and the wide variety of designs produced in small batches allow vendors to quickly respond to changing fashion trends and customers' needs without the risk of carrying large inventories (Kim and Shin 2000). This kind of shift leads to the flexible production and accumulation that critical geographers, such as David Harvey (1989), observed in industrial cities and global outsourcing systems.[7] The recently developing fast-fashion industry—as exemplified by the "retail revolution" of such American and European clothing companies as Zara, H&M, and Forever 21—has pushed accelerated flexible production to extremes, by reducing the time between design and production and delivering new items twice a week to the storefront. Yet, Dongdaemun's fast on-site production urges us to more closely examine its decentralized process of flexibilization and the remaking of place in a local site that embodies the transition from global mass manufacturing to fast fashion.

In this local-level fast-fashion industry, quick turnover is even faster in the intricate networks consisting of small-scale factories and wholesalers, quite frequently connected by family-owned networks. Besides South Koreans, significant numbers of groups are present, including East Asian, Central Asian, and Russian traders. These transnational actors make frequent short trips to Korea to conduct business in the marketplace and often carry by hand business contracts and goods across borders, which gives them a reason to keep their businesses' scale small. Many Koreans in Central Asia and Russia have developed informal ethnic business networks, and a small Russian street has formed near Dongdaemun. Japanese vendors are mostly individual online and off-line retailers and used clothes traders, who do not have the scale to reach out to more remote locations, such as western China or South Asia. Chinese traders have formed larger systems of networks and connect with such fast-fashion manufacturing hubs as Guangzhou. These long-standing networks have shaped the heterogeneous transnational landscape of Dongdaemun market since the 1960s,[8] along with occasional, hasty speculative real-estate investments by large-scale foreign financial capital.[9]

It is notable that the 1997 Korean financial crisis and the subsequent transition to a consumer society increased the informal labor market, including street vendors and small-scale garment factories in Dongdaemun (Noritake 2009). In the garment manufacturing of South Korea, 90 percent of businesses are small scale, employing fewer than ten workers. More specifically, small-scale factories with five employees or fewer compose 76.5 percent of the industry. These types of small-scale businesses are in many cases home based and have increased their portion of the sector between 2011 and 2013. Within Seoul, more than 50 percent of the garment businesses are closely connected to Dongdaemun and the adjacent area (Korean Apparel Industry Institute 2003, 11). In many cases, as I illustrate in chapters 1–3, manufacturing workers are also self-employed people whose sense of self includes identifying as manual laborers, sewing masters, and microentrepreneurs. The market also has a wide range of retailers, from renowned global apparel companies, Korean domestic companies, and department stores to microretail shops that are run by online bloggers who find unique clothes in the market and sell them in their virtual stores.

It is these independently contracted and small-scale actors—the quick-service driver, the online blogger, the home-factory workers, who materialize the market's speed and flexibility through inconsistent logics, practices, hierarchies, and desires. That is, flexible production is far from a coherently organized system following the standardized rationale set out by the dominant corporation as was once assumed by the literature of flexible production. Anna Tsing's (2009) suggestion to shift the focus from commodity-chain to supply-chain capitalism is highly relevant to arguments concerning the intricate network of Dongdaemun's subcontract system. Global outsourcing networks are increasingly comprised of multiple independent subcontractors and organized by subjective and cultural dimensions, as Tsing (2009, 150) argues, rather than a vertically hierarchical company structure. Within this diversity, flexibility is not a singular system through which a dominant company expands to the world but rather a descriptive word for new styles and subjects, producing economic diversities. Recent anthropological studies of the garment industry take this a step further by focusing on the complex configurations of fast fashion and flexible production. For instance, Nellie Chu (2016, 198–202) describes the "craft-like mode of mass production" in the case of fast fashion in southern China; Elizabeth Krause (2018) explores the social landscape of Italy's fast fashion changed by Chinese migrant laborers; and Christina Moon (2014) emphasizes the ethnic and religious implications of Asian American fast-fashion firms.

I also endeavor to shift away from an analytical framing of "fast fashion" as a fixed type of flexible production and circulation and instead look at it as a set of practices in which we can see the multiple and incongruent spatiotemporal dimensions of not only commodities but also those who are invested in the various registers of garment production and circulation. The extension of fast-paced productivity into the nighttime hours exemplifies one such dimension of people working and being in Dongdaemun. Dongdaemun is not merely a fast-paced marketplace; it is also a central site for the landscape of Seoul as a 24-hour city. The dense flow of people through the market both day and night fuels the fast-paced garment production and nonstop circulation of people and things.

The Temporality of Work

Stitching the 24-Hour City considers both individual performances and narratives of work. Lived experiences of working with clothes and the life of work itself extend beyond work hours, produce a surplus (sometimes unexpectedly), and are always more complex than a simple job description within the dominant frame of wage labor. Feminist theorist Weeks (2011), in her work on the politics of work, calls for an attentiveness to "its spaces, relations, and temporalities; its physical, affective, and cognitive practices; its pains and pleasures" (2011, 18). I take this lesson to resist imposing a "protagonist" of formal wage labor in this marketplace where predominant numbers of women simultaneously take multiple social and economic roles; and I value the "self-description" (18) workers share as they make sense of what they do rather than categories of occupation. In the narratives that I engage with in this book, people sometimes defend their work as valuable but also sometimes deny the value and capacity of their work. The self-description of their activities, skills, and motivations shows the dissident relationships that these workers have with the history of the market and the South Korean economy, as well as the widespread and individually experienced insecurity of work and life. By giving ethnographic attention to these narratives, I hope to vividly convey my interlocutors' sense of affective and material attachment to their work and in turn show how their work is not merely contained in the ideological underpinnings of time or merely extracted by the logic of capitalist acceleration. Rather, I show the act of working *in and on time* as Laura Bear (2014, 20) suggests, through their interactions with the material production and circulation, the limits and habituation of the body, their tools and skills, and "coordination of diverse rhythms and representation."

Garment manufacturing is one of the most marginalized professions in Korea and around the globe, typically performed in sweatshops by working-class women. The stitching was often considered as something one can learn quickly without much investment of time, despite the fact that it eventually takes a long training period for one to become an independent seamstress (Green 1996; Bonacich 1994).[10] The image of the female factory worker, known as *yeogong* (factory women) or *gongsuni* (a denigrating term roughly translated as "factory girl"), became the symbol of the arduous labor of the 1970s in Korea and its narratives (Barraclough 2012; W. Kim 2005), characterized by her repetitive, mind-numbing work for long hours in exploitative conditions.[11] Yet many workers that I interviewed remained in Dongdaemun despite the unchanging conditions of low-wage work, and these resilient workers have now accumulated thirty-five to forty years of experience in sewing.

In the 2000s, garment workers are further marginalized by the cultural logic of the knowledge economy that presumes gendered and classed notions of garment work as being *temporally obsolete* (Park 2019a). As I briefly discussed above, South Korea's new economic plan in 2008 promoted the idea that young designers would produce a moral, legitimate, and controlled form of knowledge and, most importantly, that they would be different from the image of undereducated designers of the informal marketplace, like Jiyoung. The image of the young, college-educated, white-collar worker was intended to provide a sharp contrast to the image of the aging, blue-collar manufacturing workers, making South Korea's historical transition *legible* and *tangible* in the next phase of the economy (Park 2019a).[12] As such, the marginalization of garment work is not only classed and gendered but also *temporal* and *spatial*, in that it positions current garment-stitching workers at the margins of the contemporary economy and presents them as representing the past.[13] While lower-class, "industrial women warriors" have become a symbol of Korea's *past* developmental growth, similar figures are now taking up that role in remote offshore locations.

Within this context, one of the analytic goals of this book is to consider the multiplicity of these seemingly self-apparent boundaries of occupation. In contrast to dominant narratives of space-time, this ethnography presents the persistent presence of garment workers and the continuity between their work with designers and traders. Thuy Tu's (2011) ethnography shows that sewing and designing are intimately connected with kinship and family business among Asian American migrant families. The prestige economy of fashion, however, remains out of reach for these workers, a paradox she calls "a cultural economy of distance" between production and consumption (Tu 2011, 26–28). Here I also show that the categories of manufacturing and designing work are interwoven and porous because work sites are physically proximate and closely related by kinship, sisterhood, and friendship (chapters 2 and 3).

The long duration of work in the 24-hour market disrupts the division between work time and nonwork time. Garment workers and designers typically work from 9 a.m. to 9 p.m., and very often much longer, while vendors work at all different times of the day and night. If wholesale or retail vendors also design their own clothes, their work and sleeping hours are irregularly mixed throughout the day. The predominance of self-employment in outsourcing networks and the continued devaluation of manual labor drove out workers to the constant and unending work of the 24-hour market. In accounts of socially arranged and organized time, labor has been a prominent site for analysis. However, the analyses tend to focus on the fragmentation of daily schedule and prolonged duration of worktime that have engulfed workers' whole lives. In these accounts, the temporal aspects of labor are often depicted as an abstract apparatus for the governance and biopolitics of the physical aspects of labor.

In exploring the labor side of this 24-hour cycle, this book highlights the affective production of people who are positioned differently in the market—individuals coordinating efficient production, competing with each other, and working in and occupying the space together. I am indebted to feminist anthropologists and geographers who highlighted the question of "working shifts" in a way that complicates the divisions between the equal and unequal. Beyond exploring a dichotomy between consumers and laborers working in the nighttime economy, feminist studies of women's work also question the very division of labor time as juxtaposed to leisure time, a public sphere separated neatly from the private sphere, as well as the paradox of "freedom." For instance, Anne Allison's in-depth fieldwork in Tokyo's hostess clubs (Allison 1994) documented the expectations and experiences of Japanese hostesses, as well as the male customers to whom they catered. Allison criticizes the notion of a simple transition from productive time to leisure time by highlighting the way that work is masked by leisurely family-like corporate culture and women's emotional labor. Reena Patel (2010) also discusses the "temporal mobility" experienced by customer call center representatives in India, indicating that time both enabled and restricted their social mobility. Likewise, this book approaches night as a temporalized social space. It explores the nighttime economy of Dongdaemun as being closely connected to the daytime cycles of production and circulation via intimate networks (chapter 2 and 3); produced by a spectacle of working bodies, energy, and hard-work ethics (chapter 1); and as city development branded and sold as a form of urban regeneration (chapter 5).

While undefined and prolonged and different from a demarcated workday, the time of work in this 24-hour context is full of multifaceted practices of production. By actively incorporating "life" in an exploration of the time and space of work, especially as it pertains to women's work, this book sheds light on what is happening in and on the boundaries of unstructured work and wage labor (Folbre 2004; Leccardi 1996). With this busy schedule, workers produce more value than what they are numerically compensated for, and their experiences extend beyond work-time activities. In looking at Italian families in the garment industry, Sylvia Yanagisako (2012, 16–18) has aptly suggested that intimacy and affect have been studied in the context of immaterial labor in the service and knowledge industry, creating a binary of immaterial and industrial labor. While people in Dongdaemun do their work, they simultaneously care for others, create friendship and love, become visible to or part of a crowd, and animate others and themselves. All of this work unsettles the distinction between wage labor and unwaged labor (Denning 2010, 79–82) and contributes to extending and reproducing the viability, vitality, and commodity value of this urban marketplace.

Problematizing Speed

When discussing the speed of work in the market, I have intentionally used the term "fast-pace" to capture the heterogeneous intricacies of work and implication in the politics of time. The way people narrate their own experiences, workers are situated within the local context in which critiques of speed are formed and practiced, especially through labor activism and urban planning. These political problematizations of speed strongly resonate with scholarly inquiries into the speed of capitalist economic and social processes.

Analyses abound that critique the synchronization of bodies and machinery in modern times. The extent to which one is physically subjected to machine speeds has been used to evaluate work's innate meaning and values. The critique of the temporality of industrial capitalism is that machines synchronize and co-ordinate labor throughout the production process, subsuming the human body, mind, and socialization to the rhythms of technology. Optimal efficiency is achieved when the tempo of the machines, human motions, and even the con-sciousness of workers are all attuned to a unified pace of production, expressing the alienation of labor via *time*.

The problematization of the speed of production orients us to human experi-ences of work by revealing the structured orchestration of time regimes that dis-cipline labor. E. P. Thompson's (1967) classic historiography of the nineteenth century shows how the rise of numeric time, its external technological and tech-nocratic formulation, and the cultural processes that promote the internalization of emerging regimes of power transformed agricultural workers into productive industrial laborers. Postindustrial theorists further this critique by emphasizing the destandardization of time; the bodily disciplines in time operate for individ-ual bodies in the form of the biopower of just-in-time labor (Pamela 2003, 293–95) or the permeation of the military logic of discipline into media, the public sec-tor, and advocate groups in virtual real time (Virilio and Bratton 2006, 71–72). These works theorize that there is no way out of this tyranny of abstracted time. David Harvey's (1989) treatise on time-space compression and the shrinking globe brought attention to 24-7 city spaces, where the accelerating paces of productivity never stop. For example, the synchronization of working hours be-tween cities scattered across the globe eliminates those unproductive hours dur-ing the day and night that are necessitated by the human biological need to eat, sleep, and rest. Similarly, the temporal coordination *within* cities that keeps them open 24-7 eliminates nonworking hours (and, by extension, nonconsumer hours) as people eat, shop, work, and relax beyond the constraints of the clock.[14]

The macro analytic framework of time-space compression is useful for under-standing speed as a technology of global capitalism. However, this powerful ab-stracting device simultaneously obscures the heterogeneous activities of individuals and their networks as they go about their work, limiting our ability to analyze the implication of these performances in the production and experience of time. As much as speed itself, "speed theory" and the overreliance on it as a critique for late capitalism also fail to consider the lived experiences of time. Concerning the "problem of speed," Sarah Sharma (2014, 15) argues that speed theorists have simplified the experience of accelerating everyday life, thereby ignoring the temporal differences that she sees as critical to producing social inequality. Similarly, Judy Wajcman (2014) discusses the "time-pressure paradox," which she defines as the myths and misconceptions about high-speed society and our contemporary feelings of hurriedness. Wajcman suggests that paying attention to people's experiences of pace, cycles, intensity, and temporal density offers a more nuanced understanding of capitalist time than a narrow conceptualization of time as numeric velocity or the length of working hours.[15] To understand the subjective experiences of time and the multiple diversions of chronotopes, I claim to call attention not only to the political economy and technological conditions and representations of time but also to the way speed *matters as a problem* in the particular local context.

This ethnography is grounded in a specific location, Dongdaemun market, in which the emphasis on speed has an impact on notions of labor, market, and the city. Here, general features of the Korean industrial and postindustrial economy and urban space, as well as the local histories and senses of time, are all a part of people's experience of work. The paces of production and circulation are intertwined with temporal implications for intimate space and relationships, gender divisions and negotiations, and one's sense of mobility and work in the city (chapters 1, 2, and 3). At the same time, in the intricate outsourcing system of self-employed workers from stitching workers to traders, the speed of work during these long hours is directly associated with the workers' everyday income in cash. As a result, the emphasis on speed has become a fetishistic ethos that people pursue and impose on each other. Accordingly, for a local actor like MANI, speed is not only a problem for labor politics but also a moral problem that workers themselves perpetuate through their quick work. Whether they are employed in a factory or work as self-employed designers, laborers who effectively embody the fast working tempo demanded by their industry paradoxically hinder the efforts of labor organizations that aim to ameliorate this very problem (chapter 4).

Moreover, "compression" itself is tied with historical awareness, critiques of the political economy, and knowledge production in South Korea. Here, I am not just repeating the widespread commentary on the tenacious cultural ethos of *ppalli ppalli* (fast, fast) that is more than frequently raised as being typical in South Korea and sometimes as a flattened causality for various kinds of social phenomena. The rapidity of social change and its attendant problems have been a common theme in the academic discourse of Korea. Korea is often noted as being an interesting place to explore issues of time-space compression, and scholars of Korea emphasize the notion of compression as a distinctive characteristic of "modern" Korea, and

East Asian societies in general (Robinson and Shin 1999). Historians and social scientists note that the rapid expansion of capitalism within South Korea after the end of the Second World War took place at an unprecedented rate (Koo 2001) and was a unique cultural indicator of Korea's postcolonial and post–Cold War modernity (K.-S. Chang 2010; H. Cho 1998). As the sociologist Kyung-Sup Chang (2010, 30) noted, "South Koreans have experienced Westerners' historical development of two or three centuries over merely three or four decades." Fast change was a primary feature of the state-led development projects that executed authoritative planning to expedite Korea's transition from a periphery to a semiperiphery economy. This top-down emphasis on rapidity became the most well-known theme of intellectual and critical inquiry into Korean society. Sociologists and anthropologists have pointed out that it has also become a cultural idiom for venture capitalists (Chung 2003), and film and literature critiques are interested in how time-space compression unfolds (therefore, "decompresses") in text (Martin-Jones 2007). Time-space compression was thought by those who study Korean society to have generated broader structural problems such as class, gender, and age disparities (Abelmann 2003; Kendall 2002), brutal and destructive urbanization (W. B. Kim 1999); as well as increasing individual and collective mental health and suicide (Crabbe 2014).

Dongdaemun captures the way developmentalism becomes a discursive and material matter not only for a social and intellectual critique but also for civil activists and urban planners as a marker of the "past." Activists look to "development" as evidence for how far we have come in the present, and where will be headed in the future. As feminist scholars of South Korea have critiqued, "compressed modernity" is also a narrative and an epoch-making concept in postcolonial knowledge production.[16] In chapters 4 and 5, I directly address how the problematization of speed itself is a conduit of new market and urban projects articulating neoliberal market logic and public value. The critical point I make is that even these kinds of alternative actions that alter and envision a new temporality are entangled in dissident paces of practice, hope, and anxiety.

Ultimately, this ethnography is primarily concerned with what it takes for people to enable speedy production and circulation in particular contexts and also how they incorporate the critique of speed in the ways they make sense of their own work. This ethnography aligns with recent works in cultural studies, geography, and anthropology that endeavor to attenuate the totalizing tendency of theories of speed, which reinforce the notion of high speed as the universal antithesis of human liberty. More specifically, I see the speed of work and markets as a flow, broken into short paces and cycles that are implicated in subjective experience and historical awareness. I aim to see space-time contradictions of capitalism as multiple and mediated through human labor in and of time (Bear et al. 2015).

I understand flow in both analytic and ethnographic terms. When we think of a river or stream, it has multiple currents: some short, some backward, some slow, some fast. Similar to a stream, in the market these layers are not separated from each other but come together to form the big, seemingly fast currents of commodity production, circulation, and consumption. Hugh Raffle's (2002) notion of the "flow of becoming" imagines "flow" as being made up of different types of water in terms of direction, length, quality, and depth. The flow is transformed by constant interactions with people, forests, rivers, and animals, all of which compose the stream in different locations and at different times. Likewise, for my interlocutors, shared moments with family, friendship, and sisterhood, endurance and collapse of marriages, and embodied paces of work interweave the ceaseless motion of the sewing machine. Retroactive nostalgia, moral support, and stagnant aspirational and spiritual daily cycles saturate this marketplace imagined as a site for the expedited future to come. The temporal analyses of this ethnography ultimately reveal the "affects and ethics that inform capitalist time" to precisely understand human practices shaping space-time (Bear 2014, 22). It is undeniable that Dongdaemun is characterized by a rapid flow and that a notion of homogeneous time is already implicated in the prevailing understanding of speed. Yet, by revealing how the pace of production arises as a problem for both theorists and my ethnographic subjects alike, I challenge reproducing a singular critique and teleological explanation of these multiple paces.

Catching Up the Pace in Fieldwork

This book is based on extensive fieldwork in Seoul, Korea, between 2008 and 2010, as well as intermittent short fieldwork. Over the years, I conducted participant observation in factories, shop floors, and MANI's classrooms and offices. While there I shadowed and sometimes conducted interviews with factory workers and Korean and foreign merchants and designers throughout the marketplace. I also conducted interviews with various individuals located throughout the market, including online shopping mall owners, off-line retail store staff and owners, and staff members of merchants' organizations.

At first, I was overwhelmed by the marketplace's speed and the intensity of work, and then by the way people spoke about it. Indeed, the quick pace that characterizes Dongdaemun materially and discursively saturates the place. For example, speed even arose as an issue in the way I conducted my interviews. The first person I interviewed, Namsu, a wholesaler of women's clothing, stopped the interview to ask if I was from Chungcheong-do, a western region in Korea in which the local dialect is characterized by a relaxed and soft drawl. Brushing off the question,

I replied that I was from Seoul. Eventually, Namsu discovered my age. Startled, he said, "Now I get it! You are older than I expected! That's why you speak so slowly! [Naiga saenggakboda jom inne!]" I had never been told that I speak slowly before, but it seemed that my conversation style stood out to the workers in Dongdaemun. Namsu advised me, "You might want to speak a bit faster because people are very impatient here and might not give you their full attention." At first, I wondered if Namsu was implying that he was annoyed; however, I quickly realized he was both joking and making a sincere suggestion.

Different tempos of life and work marked the differences and connections that I had with my interlocutors. They often teased me for lagging behind in my life: I ate slowly and talked slowly, I was woefully behind the fashion trends, I had not yet married nor had a child (despite my apparently ticking biological clock), and despite my age, I was still a student with no income (at the time). For some of my interlocutors, the duration of my ethnographic fieldwork seemed too long and loose. The slow tempo of my work and my demeanor for them was a social privilege (McLuhan and Lewis 1994). For others, it made sense that I kept coming back to taking time to learn about their work as their work is not at all easily graspable and full of complexities. The paces of biological, physical, and social clocks emerged in various ways as we talked about work and shaped my relationship with them.

Although Namsu was concerned about my ability to fit in, in Dongdaemun, he was kind enough to allow me to shadow his employees and introduce me to others. I made entries in multiple locations in the market through meeting people like Namsu. Once I made entries, I expanded the pool of interview participants, sometimes relying on the intricately connected network of garment production and distribution (chapter 2) through family, friends, and sisters. During my fieldwork, I was also fortunate enough to hold a volunteer position at MANI through which I met garment workers, factory owners, traders, activists, and other experts, such as instructors and university professors, in the field of garment making and fashion.

The nature of this research heavily relied on extensive participant observation in addition to individual interviews with my interlocutors. One of my strategies to better access, first, and also understand the embodied paces and incongruent temporality of work was to be there to experience and encounter them in person. In Dongdaemun, every individual from a staff member in MANI to the shopping mall owners was extremely busy. I would take on the work that others were too busy for, such as assisting stitching workers in factories, organizing and taping packages on the wholesale shop floor, cleaning classrooms, making photocopies, and taking pictures in MANI's classes. Occasionally, I also engaged in writing newsletters, research papers, budget reports, and review reports for MANI's projects and other institutions in Dongdaemun. However, my contribution to their work remained peripheral, and my interlocutors jokingly called me "unskilled labor with a high education" (*gohangnyeok jeogeup gisulja*). Unlike my interlocutors, I was the one with flexible schedule, able to help on demand. Working together helped me to find room in their extremely busy work schedule. In this way, I was able to learn about work through working and eventually began to experience sharing and conversing about paces of work and life.

The fieldwork was to work with and *walk with* them rather than walking into their lives, as Jo Lee and Tim Ingold (2006) pointed out in their essay "Fieldwork on Foot." As the beginning of this introduction described, I could only accompany my interlocuters while they were working or walking somewhere, leaving me to stumble over pauses, delays, and detours or catching up, without being able to perfectly synchronize them. And it was through walking together, literally and metaphorically, that I shared with my interlocutors the pedestrian pace, the turnaround of one design item, fashion trend cycles, paydays and budget cycles, and the sense of bodily aging. The bureaucratic time of various government and funding institutions around MANI's project, as well as the time frame of massive urban planning projects, also accentuated the duration of my fieldwork.

These projects reveal the multiple notions of the Korean word *sijang*, or market. The morpheme, *jang*, in the word *sijang*, refers to both a social arena where interactions and activities take place and a particular geographic place. Accordingly, quotes and analyses in the book often address colloquial uses of the market and Dongdaemun market, such as "going to market" (*sijang e-gada*, going to Dongdaemun wholesale and retail shopping plazas), "market clothes" (*sijang ot*, the clothes often produced without recognizable brand name that has become the synonymous with Dongdaemun clothes), or "market logic" (*sijang nolli*, the general mechanism of abstract market economy, prevalent in the critique of fast-paced work in Dongdaemun). The problematics set by the government and the civil organization reflect and articulate ideas and opportunities about the course of economic activities and relations with narratives of the rapidity of economy and urban history.[17] These ideas and opportunities form a node in different temporal and value networks (Miyazaki 2003) and are channeled into MANI's and the state's economic and urban projects.

MANI offered a particularly provocative site for research because it foregrounded a countermarket experiment. MANI connected differently situated actors in Dongdaemun, including former activists for labor unions and social democratization movements, social workers, workers in various registers of garment making and trading, co-op leaders, and new entrepreneurs. Gradually, the practice of MANI itself became my object of study, as a way to understand how people's problematization of speed had spawned a new market, thereby shaping and altering the social and time scale of the market. At the same time, MANI was a social setting that exposed my interlocutors to the questions of work and encouraged them to talk about their own narratives. Consequently, conversations naturally emerged on the issues of labor, social activism, and new market experiments. The NGO's problematization of time, along with the workers' discussion of their self-realization of the value of their work, helped me to form my own analyses of the meaning of time, speed, and work in ways that I would have missed outside of the NGO.

Outline of the Book

Stitching the 24-Hour City is immersed in people's narratives and lived experiences of work and the city space. With this perspective, the book argues that the market's accelerated, unceasing productivity relies heavily on and coconstitutes each actor's affective and embodied attachments to commodities, their own labor practices, and other workers rather than disabling these attachments. These attachments give new meanings to their subjectively and collectively imagined work, redefining the boundaries between creative design and piracy, between intimate and instrumental relationships, and between material and immaterial labor. As people become more aware of and respond to the problematization of their work through efforts like those of MANI's and the state's projects, the presence and contradictions of these attachments become more apparent and complicate labor and urban politics.

Part 1 focuses on *speed as experience* by detailed attention to the paces, cycles, and courses of daily work and personal lives that are intertwined with the material speed of commodity production and circulation.

Bringing us to the nighttime landscape of Dongdaemun, chapter 1, "Affective Crowds and Making the 24-Hour City," opens the book with snapshots of the nighttime (and dawn-time) city as it is intertwined with the fast pace of productivity for twenty-four hours. I highlight how my interlocutors' intensive in-person interactions, mobilities in space, and aspirations result in animating the nighttime city both for others and themselves. Despite their different trajectories and tempos of work, people in the market intentionally and unintentionally embody the hard-work ethics, affect, and spectacle for others in the 24-hour city.

Chapter 2, "Intimate Networks," illustrates how working people build relationships with their spouses, children, siblings, and friends within and alongside their labor, interweaving these intimate relationships with the market's manufacturing, wholesaling, and retailing networks. The emphasis on intimacy unsettles perceived dichotomies between the inside and outside of the home, factory, and market. We see how people's practices in the market are simultaneously acts of caring, reproduce and disturb gender relations, and provide avenues to tactically fulfil or avoid family duties. I argue that intimacy and the market are coproduced and mobilize one another and that this process makes the fast pace and viability of Dongdaemun market possible.

The fast-fashion clothes are newly "created" but are also perceived as "imitations." The commodities range from nonbrand clothes to explicit knock-offs appropriating famous brand logos. While rapid design and stitching have allowed Dongdaemun to thrive, they have also produced a perception that the work done there cannot be original or a labor of love. Chapter 3, "Passionate Imitation," illuminates how designers and seamstresses frame or accept their work as "imitations" yet still perform this work with passion, attachment, and care, unintentionally amplifying the range of meanings that "imitation" carries, without attempting to include their work within the authoritative regime of copyrightable creativity. Passionate imitation is an ethnographic lens through which we account for the emotional and affective aspects of fast-paced economic processes and rework the critique of time and work.

Part 2 of the book explores how labor activists and the city government engaged with the problematization of speed as a place-based and historically situated problem and as a legacy of the old logics of growth-centered, state-led economic and urban developmentalism that were popular during the 1960s and 1990s. The embodied and imagined presence of "garment work" in these future-oriented NGO and urban projects reveals heterogenous attachments and vitalities that paradoxically persist and alter the current time-space of the city and marketplace.

Chapter 4, "Redirecting the Future," discusses how MANI, a civil organization, takes part in the legacy of labor activism of Dongdaemun but also encapsulates the new market logic of a social enterprise. The chapter illustrates the practices of various actors who participated in MANI's experiment to "slow down" the sped-up production and consumption as a way of political and moral critiques of what they see as problems in Dongdaemun and the garment industry. However, the project shows that the social enterprise that attempts to counteract the market's speed shares a similar capitalist logic about speed (assuming that a singular speed is a vehicle for surplus value) and developmental temporality (believing that by controlling speed we can improve the future). The chapter argues that the engineering of a "slow" pace faces its own complexities, due to incongruent logics, attachments, and investments by different actors, has ultimately fostered and halted this new market project.

Zooming out to the city again, chapter 5, "Pacing the Flow," discusses the macrolevel transformation of the landscape that attempted to discursively and physically create the slow pace of the city, in an attempt to alter the previous urban pursuit of growth-centered, sped-up urban lives. This chapter traces the recent changes through the perspectives of three women and their sense of inadequacy facing the rapid renewals of the landscape. As former and current seamstresses and labor activists, their memories of work, life, and activism are entangled in Dongdaemun and challenge the linear and developmental logic of the urban history.

In synthesizing the book's overall argument, the conclusion returns to Oksun's story, which opened the book in the prologue. The story here conveys the ethnographic challenge of analyzing the problem of speed: inasmuch as our critique of labor targets the abstracting force of speed, it is also hard to translate people's experiences and feelings without using the language of abstracting, alienating speed. I reiterate my argument that human practices to relate with and build attachment to others, commodities, and to work itself constitute the very dynamic of speed and accelerated, unceasing productivity. In doing so, the practices inevitably create a flow of life that is dense and messy and that simultaneously sustains and contradicts the speed of the market and the city.

Part 1

SPEED AS EXPERIENCE

AFFECTIVE CROWDS AND MAKING THE 24-HOUR CITY

At around 9 or 10 p.m., all the roads surrounding Dongdaemun market start to jam. Quick-service motorbikes and minivans with big packages, lines of tourist buses with Chinese and Japanese characters on their exteriors, and commuter buses and cars fill the streets. The packages contain freshly made clothes from stitching factories and finishing factories in adjacent neighborhoods. Motorbikes enter the district, a dense cluster of glaring and flamboyant neon signs in the dark. The whole area, full of light, noise, music, and busy movement of people has been repeatedly covered in tour guides and foreign media. Several major wholesale buildings typically operate from 8 or 9 p.m. to 8 a.m., while the retail buildings typically operate from 10 a.m. to 5 a.m. the following day. With all fifteen wholesale and retail buildings utilizing different, overlapping business hours for twelve to eighteen hours, the area is running twenty-four hours a day.

The wholesale market reaches peak activity from 9 p.m. to 2 a.m., and the streets in front of the buildings and stores are packed with cars and motorbikes from everywhere in Korea—wholesale buyers rush to get necessary items at night, so they can sell the items immediately the following day. Along the dense grids of narrow hallways, hundreds of stores line the floors, where wholesalers talk and haggle with their buyers, sometimes yelling at each other. The retail malls across the street replicate this style of wholesaling—myriads of commodities and stores, informal communications and haggling, and the excitement of unusual shopping hours. Besides the relatively cheap price of clothes in various styles, the urban experience at Dongdaemun market has become a source of excitement for consumers and tourists, who enjoy shopping and music events in front of the

FIGURE 1.1. Crowds gather for a nighttime performance in front of the retail shopping plaza at around 9 p.m.

Photo by the author.

shopping plazas (figure 1.1) and float to the wholesale buildings, weaving through street vendors, snacking, and navigating the messy and dynamic landscape that the nearby manufacturing and distribution processes create (figure 1.2).

This is the nighttime scene, the counterpart to the typical daytime routine that I followed with Jiyoung at the beginning of the introduction. Dongdaemun's ceaseless production and circulation have become an iconic symbol of the dense energy and people of the nightscape of Seoul. It is the spectacle of goods, people, and their sped-up movement in the space. The packages are rarely organized in

FIGURE 1.2. Nighttime Dongdaemun, around the wholesale marketplace buildings at approximately 12:30 a.m.

Photo by Euirock Lee.

boxes or containers; rather, they arrive in chunks of plastic wrap and duct tape piled up in the shop fronts (figure 1.3). Each store, a small cubicle of about 3.3–5.0 m² (often pejoratively called "chicken cage shops," *dakjang maejang* in Korean), and the narrow corridors soon become cluttered with these bundles. They are usually carried on bodies—of the quick-service bikers or porters who can navigate the narrow alleys, corridors, and stairs within and around the buildings. After a while, clothes are repackaged and piled in shop fronts and corridors again—now in even smaller bundles, typically in what the workers call *daebong* (large plastic shopping bags), with *jangkki* (receipt) taped to them and names of the store scribbled on the bags. As retailers and buyers move fast from one store to the other, instead of carrying them all, they have the wholesalers make the package. The packages, in a couple hours, are handpicked by a quick-service person, who delivers them to their stores, or by *jigekkun* (a courier using a *jige*) to the bus station. On the side of the bus station, there are Korean Post Office booths and other private courier companies who accommodate same-day shipping directly from the marketplace.

While not readily apparent in this wholesale and retail landscape, the production labor—including the work of seamstresses and designers—of the garment

FIGURE 1.3. Nighttime Dongdaemun, by the wholesale marketplace buildings at approximately 12:30 a.m.

Photo by the author.

manufacturing networks has a strong presence, instead of being merely contained within a factory, shopping mall, or plaza or restricted to daytime hours. The intense and swift cumulation of goods and the mobility of people who trade them evidence the sped-up production and circulation throughout the whole day and physically, materially, and affectively tie the nighttime space into the 24-hour cycle. This feature makes Dongdaemun particular and challenges the generalization of the nighttime city by framing it as place of transition from industrial to postindustrial urban processes, often characterized by the entertainment districts in a city, such as the clusters of nightclubs, pubs, restaurants, or galleries that symbolize post-Fordist leisure and a consumer economy catering to the urban creative class.[1] The unconventional time-space of shopping and loitering in Dongdaemun became attractive to buyers and tourists precisely because the marketplace merges with the time and space of manufacturing and distribution.

The marketplace is an open, public space where vendors, customers, tourists, and garment workers merge in urban crowds twenty-four hours a day. The crowd does not merely reflect the number of individual nighttime activities: the presence of these people itself can attract more people to join. Sinhye, a seamstress working in her own home-factory[2] in a nearby neighborhood, occasionally walked across the street to the shopping mall areas after the long hours of stitching on the sewing machine all day. Sinhye recalled her past experience selling clothes to retail customers in the nighttime wholesale market, saying, "I felt like I am alive, that I am working for something, being part of these busy people working really hard in the glittering and colorful lights. . . . . I am not alone, working hard and struggling for life." Walking along the allies of Dongdaemun Sinhye tires feel the excitement and energy of the marketplace. Dongsu Go, an officer of the Information Center for Foreign Buyers, described his fascination with the market in the following way: "Whenever I feel lazy, or I find my wife and children are complaining about life, I take them to the market to refresh our minds by seeing the dynamic scene of people working at night."

This "dynamic scene of people working at night" or the light and energy that Sinhye pursued was common in the descriptions of Dongdaemun that I frequently encountered during my fieldwork: casual chatting with others, reading on social networks and blog posts, and viewing in media representations. Sometimes people recommend you go to Dongdaemun during the peak wholesale time to experience this vibrancy, even though it is a bad time for individual retail customers, who get ignored or rejected for shopping. This vibrancy and excitement over the dynamic movement of people attract increasing consumer and tourist interest and intensify the commodity value of the place itself. This chapter further delves into the varied aspirations and practices in the marketplace to understand how this energy expands and affects other working bodies, as well as the spatial and temporal relationship they maintain with the marketplace.

The atmosphere of the market's brightness and energy comes from people's affective reactions and interactions: the immediate sense of the presence of other people working and moving at a fast pace during the time when other parts of the city are dormant. One's own movement and capacity to come out and be part of the people form a circulation and a motion that creates "public feelings" or *ordinary affect* (Stewart 2007). The geographer Mike Crang (2001) has argued that being-in-the-world itself is a performative production of temporalized space. The lines and motion, which people inscribe and chart daily or even hourly, create the sense of rhythm and repetition that connects with ideas of routinization in space (Crang 2001, 200). The ones who occupy the city space are not merely human bodies, but also a particular "atmosphere" emerges from these bodies and their interactions. It is this kind of affective atmosphere, not just a structural pattern, that constructs the urban night (Gandy 2017; Hatfield 201; Shaw 2014).[3] In a similar vein, I see the work of my interlocutors in this chapter not just as merely an activity of buying, trading, and selling commodities; but rather, in their own practice, interactions, and mobility, they are acting on and shaping the particular time-space of the night in Dongdaemun. Throughout this chapter, I focus on how working people not only conduct their work in this period, but how their presence materially and affectively transforms this market at night (or dawn) into a new sort of time-space of aspiration: their imagined and physical presence is recognized, publicized, and "felt" as a sign of vibrancy, energy, and a mode of being "productive" for people. The value the people produce in this space is much larger than the shift work during extended business hours, and it is a value that is difficult to count within the frame of defined job descriptions and work hours. The overwhelming presence of the excessive amounts of commodities constantly being packed and unpacked, along with the value of the clothes themselves, frames the spectacle of the human bodies in motion.

The work of those people participating in this wholesale night market often involves performances in and of time, as their interactions with other traders and customers change over the course of the day. I explore, in turn, how the knowledge and energy of these interactive performances gets conveyed to and picked up by other people in the space, especially those who learn about clothes and business and turn their desire and excitement toward an entrepreneurial aspiration for their work and life. I argue that workers' close interactions, dense trajectories of mobility, and aspirations result in animating the city at dark, both for others and themselves. Their fast paces of daily work and life are not merely extended into the night; instead, they transmit these paces to others, inspiring them to participate in and expand the animated nighttime space. The chapter describes microentrepreneurs who connect the marketplace to overseas and online markets, evangelical churches that articulates commercial and religious aspirations, and the state's desire to brand the city's nightscape. Despite their different trajectories and tempos of work, people in the market intentionally and unintentionally embody the "hard-work" ethics, affect, and spectacle for others in the 24-hour city.

The Genealogy of the Night

In the early 2000s, a new term emerged to describe the lifestyle that breaks down the division between day and night, the Korean neologism *Homo naitekus*, often written with the English alphabet as *Homo nightcus*. Registered as the new vocabulary word of the year in 2003 by the National Research Council of Korea, *Homo nightcus* suggests a category of people working and playing without a division between day and night.[4] Newspaper and magazine articles, as well as posts on blogs and internet bulletin boards, have actively used the word to describe the new constructions of urban life in which nighttime activities are becoming a norm in contemporary South Korea. The term is interesting because its usage varies slightly from that of night owl (*olppaemi jok*) in that *Homo nightcus* does not clearly divide day from night.[5] Rather than being out of sync with the rest of the world, *Homo nightcus* are nighttime dwellers who are a part of their own integrated ecosystem in which they are a species with a particular life pattern that fits the environment. In a way, it insinuates the prevalent habitat of 24-hour operating Seoul and its inhabitants together rather than referring to an individual lifestyle and biorhythm.

Yet the term tends to naturalize the structural process through which people have come to work without the division of day and night. The nighttime scene in Dongdaemun is based on the specific history of the garmet industry and urban governance in South Korea. And this local history challenges a dominant and monochronic framing of 24-hour cities (Smith 2003, 567–68), that often focus only on 24-hour financial markets, the leisure industry, and extended business hours. Studies have generally been divided into those that focus on "modern" urban economies that revitalized old industrial city centers such as Manchester (Bianchini 1995; Holland and Chatterton 2003) and those that focus on "informal" nighttime marketplaces in Asia, such as Taipei or Bangkok (Hsieh and Chang 2006). Dongdaemun shows both aspects in its historical trajectory.

The rise of the nighttime wholesale market and the liberating notion of "opening the night" inherent in the nighttime market are associated with the public curfew that used to be a form of social control implemented by authoritarian military regimes. The public nighttime curfew in Seoul and Gyeonggi Province from 8:00 p.m. to 5:00 a.m. was initially implemented by the US Army in residence in 1945. This surveillance was maintained and extended nationwide in the name of national security in the Cold War context, especially under the authoritarian dictatorship of President Chung-hee Park (1961–1979). Further, in 1973, the government prohibited the usage of neon signs at night as part of its energy-saving policy.

During the late 1970s and 1980s, Dongdaemun's wholesale market competed with other Korean markets, such as Daegu or Ulsan, to become the center of the

garment industry in South Korea. To attract more retail storeowners from different regions, it started opening for business at 5:00 a.m., immediately after the
nighttime curfew was lifted.[6] The new military regime that terminated the dictatorship of Chung-hee Park finally removed the curfew in 1982 to appease the general public. Accordingly, stores in Dongdaemun competed with other markets
by opening earlier and earlier. Retail sellers came to the wholesale market at night
and then were able to get back to their hometowns early enough to start their businesses in the morning. After the curfew was lifted and other social surveillance
was loosened, the market began to open at around nine o'clock in the evening
and run until the early morning. In 1987 and 1988, the restrictions on the neon-
sign usage and late-night business operation were subsequently ended. In 1988, the
first 24-hour convenience store (*24sigan pyeonuijeom*), an indispensable component of urban life in contemporary East Asia, opened in Songpa-gu, Seoul. As
Laura Nelson (2000, 102–3) notes, the rise in consumption itself aroused fanta-
sies that Korean society had become an "advanced nation," and public discourse
touted Dongdaemun as an example of the nation's historical leap forward into a
new industrial phase and liberal social space.

The flexibilization of labor hours in the 2000s accompanied the nighttime extension of consumption sites. The transition from a six-day work week to a five-
day work week began in the context of structural adjustment and the International
Monetary Fund (IMF) bailout of South Korea. Labor activists led campaigns for
flexible and reduced work hours as a way to enhance labor conditions and quality of life in general.[7] In 2000, public schools and state institutions initiated the
five-day work week, and gradually the corporate sector followed. More service
industries joined extended nighttime operations. The newly emerging multiplex
movie theaters successfully held matinees at 7:00 a.m. (while remaining open until
2:00 a.m.), franchise coffee shops and fast food chains started staying open for
twenty-four hours, and one could even find 24-hour hair salons. Private education industries, such as foreign language classes and exercise programs, became
popular in the early morning or late afternoons, with fierce competition for customers in the precarious labor market.[8]

The emergence of the 24-hour city became emblematic of a trendy, youthful
"lifestyle" for people who wanted to take control over their daily schedules without the constraint of traditional workday hours, as suggested in the term *Homo
nightcus*. However, the perspective on nighttime expansion as a way of increasing leisure space and flexibility has raised questions of labor: who is sustaining
these extended hours so that others can have flexibility in their lives? The nonstop production and consumption have also engendered broader concerns for the
pressure to be productive and the aggravating capitalist morality of maximizing
time (for example, see Crary 2013). Once it has become a prevalent phenome-

non of the city, nighttime work could be conceived of as an "opportunity" that one's lifestyle allows (Lee and Lee 2012, 260–62), obfuscating the exploitative nature. More fundamentally, living in the 24-7 world, as Dongjin Seo (2009) and Sarah Sharma (2014) critique, is also viewed as the constant exposure to the biopolitics of time. Flexible work hours outside the nine-to-five workday and individualized forms of employment foster the imperative of ceaseless self-management and market-oriented organizations of life.

The impact of the IMF crisis and the emergence of the 24-hour city on Dongdaemun opened a new phase in the city. Opened in 1999, the first retail shopping mall, Millioré, signaled that the night of the marketplace had shifted from a time of arduous labor to a time of consumption. Replicating the wholesale style of price haggling, informal conversations, and, more importantly, nighttime operation, these new Dongdaemun-style shopping malls not only induced greater demand for clothes to be produced and sold in the marketplace but also brought the production and circulation cycle to the spectacle of the night. Similar styles of shopping malls followed, opening side by side and contributing to normalizing such nighttime entertainment for the wider population. These spaces are not operating automatically. It has become a patterned business strategy to put on cultural events—such as dance competitions, B-boy performances, or showcases of K-pop idols—in front of the main gate of shopping plazas to create an energetic atmosphere and draw attention to the malls. While shops within the malls are individually owned and managed, the shopping plazas enforce rules that require shops to remain open during certain hours in order to keep the whole building animated, without dark spaces or corners.

At the same time, as briefly mentioned in the introduction, the financial crisis and high rate of unemployment pushed a large part of the labor population to engage in contract work and small scale-businesses, which eventually provided a labor force for the outsourced, just-in-time production that the increased demand for affordable domestic clothes required. The surge in demand for these clothes also offered opportunities for young Koreans who needed a new economic niche or foreign retailers who were seeking benefits from the devalued Korean won, as I explore in this chapter. Dongdaemun's nighttime market exists as part of the terrain of accumulation and structural social disparities that does not allow any moment of slowed-down productivity. Yet, the spectacle of working bodies is not merely enacted in the service of relaxation, hedonistic indulgence, or neatly organized entertainment. The nighttime here destabilizes the simple frame of night shifts or the command of a neoliberal order. Throughout this chapter, I will pay close attention to the way the time and space of the night market become saturated by those who are a part of the garment production and circulation cycles. Their interaction with time, space, and other participants in the nighttime market ultimately creates a spectacle and affect for all that eventually further commodify the space.

Informal and Intimate

Sometimes I encountered foreign buyers who were overwhelmed by the informality of the marketplace or the huge crowds and piles of clothes filling the buildings and streets around Dongdaemun. The number of people could indeed seem to be beyond a level of optimal efficiency. If focused on the material commodity as the central point of the market's network, it would be natural to see the other elements—people, noise, lights—as excessive and the nighttime as unnecessarily "stretched out." Yet, as many ethnographies on informal and formal economies and marketplaces suggest, the affect, body, sound, or sociality of people are tightly interwoven with the calculative practices and operation of the marketplace (Bestor 2004; Wilson 2004; Zaloom 2006). Moreover, as this chapter and chapters 2 and 3 will show, the marketplace operates through personal ties and face-to-face interactions. This proximate and immanent communication happens in the public space and results in an affective atmosphere that sometimes facilitates, interferes with, or frames the material exchanges.

Working in the market all night, Chanhee tries hard to draw in customers to her women's knitwear and fur jacket store. Starting her work twenty years ago as sales staff in a wholesale store, Chanhee has successfully built up her own business, where she sometimes sells her own designs, and structures her daily life around her overnight work schedule. To draw customers' attention, Chanhee raises her voice to produce excitement and highlight the vibrancy of her store; Chanhee and many of the people with whom I spoke (whether they were storeowners, designers, sales staff members, or those who do all of the above as a one-person business) made a deliberate effort to be awake and concentrate on their work. For her, this is not structured customer service; rather, she has emotional reactions to the clothes she has invested in. She described her feelings about the pace of the market in the following way: "I think everybody here is a little bit manic in making and selling clothes; otherwise, this whole thing would not sustain. Everything is hyper, and you have to become hyper; you really invested a lot in one item, running around. And you see the immediate response; you send out two hundred pieces to your buyers, and the following night you get an order for thousands more."

This is daily life for many of the people working in the market. Chanhee's comment echoes the pleasure designers feel in making products and seeing them spread out into the world, which I will detail in chapter 3. It is the thrill, the sensation of the expansion of the material object, that they embody and feel vividly. They do this through their own performances in the nighttime market exchange or by what they consume in the market. Casual restaurants, food trucks, and small vendors selling "booster" drinks and snacks open and thrive at night, occupying the streets and alleys between the shopping mall buildings. These businesses cater not only to tourists and wholesale buyers but also to those who conduct their daily work in the marketplace.

However, it is hardly sustainable to keep up this same level of elevated energy over time. For the past fifteen years, Chanhee has learned to pace herself during different hours of operation and to respond to the changing customers. Five years ago, after many years of working for another wholesaler, Chanhee opened her own business at Cheongpyeonghwa plaza, which is open from midnight to noon. When I first visited Chanhee for an interview, she said it would be easiest for me to come between 4 and 5 a.m., since she is extremely busy between midnight and 4 a.m. She said, "You don't want to see me at night for our first meeting," and laughed. From midnight to the early morning hours, Chanhee (like the rest of the mall) was mostly engaged in commerce with wholesale buyers from different parts of Korea. By 4 a.m., most wholesalers are done with their business, although some buyers from Japan, Taiwan, or China might still do some last-minute shopping before they catch their morning flight. While 4 a.m. is still in the middle of Chanhee's business hours, these transnational buyers are winding down their shopping. Considerate of her customers' likely exhaustion, Chanhee lowers her speaking tone and generally presents herself a bit softer.

While Chanhee moderates herself to cater to her customers and adjust the atmosphere depending on the time of day, she does not entirely yield every moment. One day in the morning around 8 a.m., after having spent the whole night at the store, we got food delivered to her tiny store. The intense spicy smell from the hot soup (*jjige*) we ordered was precisely the type of smell that Murasaki, a Japanese retailer, said he distained. In the middle of our meal, a customer came to the storefront asked Chanhee if she could see more closely the white fur vest hanging on display on the back wall. Chanhee said, "Sorry, *eonni* [sister], we are eating. Could you come back a bit later?" The lady left, saying, "Oh, I am sorry. I did not know. Eat your meal, and I will come back."

I felt uncomfortable, so I asked Chanhee if she should just serve the customer rather than sending her away. I worried that the customer would think that we were not kind or welcoming to her and that she would not come back at all. Chanhee firmly said no, explaining, "Listen, if I took down the vest and brought it out to show it to her, what would happen? The fiber from the vest will shed everywhere. What if she wants to look at other things, too? That means we won't be able to get back to our meal again. But the lady can easily come back. Who suffers more for a fifteen-minute delay?" After spending some time in the nighttime market, I gradually understood that customers tolerate or would not mind this kind of inconvenience (and, not to mention, the smell), as they also know that the vendors and staff work unending hours. The affective labor with which the staff and traders conduct their business is somewhat different from the one dominated by regimented customer service often employed in the more formal sector, in which the service provider creates an atmosphere for their customers to feel better about themselves and eager to make purchases. Such an atmosphere was like "killing my own vibe as much as possible, as if there is nothing between the customer and what they buy," said Jiwoo, who was working as a salesperson at the marketplace. Once working at a department store with a dream of becoming a shop manager of a well-known designer brand, Jiwoo chose to work in Dongdaemun's wholesale market and learn how to run her own business. Instead of learning a standardized communication style and "neat and even" attitude, Jiwoo was training to master a more charismatic and casual demeanor, quick and fast communication. More informal and personal modes of interactions operate and facilitate the marketplace on the go and set up a different relationship between the product, people, and spatiotemporal contours of the market.

Throughout their working all day, the staff and traders occasionally take time themselves, which is socially shared and accepted in this night market. Chanhee's schedule was not merely the mirror opposite to a regular workday. Rather, Chanhee parceled her personal time and her work time into bundles. Sometimes Chanhee had part-time sales staff assist her, arriving after the subway begins to operate between 7:00 a.m. and midnight. During the day, Chanhee ran errands and spent some time with her child. The only way she was able to sleep was by taking multiple naps whenever possible—the pattern that many of my interlocutors in the market described in similar ways. One of the few ways Chanhee could control her daily schedule was to try to eat while working. The fifteen-minute "pause" Chanhee was able to carve out of her day was not conceived as an interruption to the flow of money and commodities in a place where workers spend more than half their life.

Personal connections, solidified trusts, or performed identities matter in the conversation and impact on the price. And the structure of exchange is changeable and depends on the interaction happening at the moment. For instance, the wholesale price is not merely determined by the bulk of purchases made. Many retailers buy one or two sample items first and wait to see the reactions of their customers before they make a big order. There is no price tag on display. Price is determined by a quick, subtle "reading" to determine what the customer does or by asking, "Where are you from?"—meaning, "Where do you have your store?" The experienced customers know to make themselves "look like" storeowners who are purchasing sample products to try out and thus get the wholesale price. In online forums and personal blogs, people share what they experience and exchange tactics for getting the best wholesale price. At the same time, the experienced sellers know at a glance, from the way customers coordinate their outfits to the way they talk and act, whether their customer is a wholesaler or a retail consumer. If the wholesalers detect that a customer is an individual retail shopper, they either suggest clothes at the more expensive retail price or simply refuse to sell in small numbers.

From learning a proper way to build rapport and negotiate price to finding the right kind of clothes of desired design and have them adjusted to a person's needs, the market requires in-person interactions for every step. Murasaki, the Japanese retailer, was no exception to this. He had started coming to Dongdaemun three years before I met him. In Japan, Murasaki and his colleagues used to go to showcases of apparel businesses and then place orders from catalogs sent to them every season, or they bought items during the nationwide apparel-maker exposition. As competition got more intense, Murasaki and his colleagues decided to find a cheaper source for imported clothes, and he began to travel to Korea. In Dongdaemun, without the promotional showcases and catalogs, he had to do a version of "window-shopping." As he explained, "It was like I needed to take steps like I was a regular [retail] shopper. I walk through the alleys, look at clothes on display, touch them to feel the texture, and make my purchases. The difference was just the amount of the order." During his first visit, Murasaki and his colleague had trouble finding deals for several days and were at the point of abandoning the whole plan of doing any business in South Korea. But on the last day of their trip, they decided to walk through every alley of the stores on the map as one final try to make their trip worthwhile. It took them almost eight hours, but they finally found a couple of wholesalers who had what they wanted in terms of design and price.

> That's how we realized that walking around, seeing clothes, and talking with the merchants is the key in Dongdaemun, and that is how everything started for us here. We expected to be able to order from Japan after the several initial visits, but we still have to come in person to walk around to choose different designs in different places. . . . I see what clothes are well liked by other buyers and look to see what other Japanese and Chinese buyers are selecting in order to figure out what I need to get. I never expected to develop friendly relationships with Korean people like I have.

After engaging in what initially seemed like a meaningless repetition, Murasaki started to discern subtle differences by exhausting the alleyways and discovering among them the one that he thought would appeal to his customers. Contrary to his initial expectation that he would work via online and telephone interactions, once having set up a contract with several wholesalers and outsourcing factories, Murasaki needed to fly to Seoul to get a variety of designs produced quickly. Over time, he built up trust with his counterparts, but for new trends and materials, he still has to make several rounds whenever he wants to find new items. This intimate engagement and immediate interactions with the people and space have become an integral part of his work.

Without a clear intention, traders and buyers like Murasaki or Chanhee make up the spectacle of "people" in the market through their own interactions and the density of their moving trajectories. There is no day-night division in their work, as they keep the fast circulation in motion transnationally. Placing orders and carrying packages day and night on his business trips to Korea, Murasaki becomes part of the crowd, continuously moving and interacting with the local market people. The emotions, aspiration, doubts, warmth, and fatigue of the night are not filtered by formalized business manners; and the necessary knowledge and sympathy that emerge in the conversations are not contained (Brennen 2004) in the showrooms and offices.[9] All of these immaterial qualities spill out to and saturate the time-space of the market and are transmitted to those who need to imitate and learn what the current traders do. Thus, it is not only the products that are on display but also the people who are buying, selling, and interacting with each other. In this way, the market is both experienced and performed.

Sped-Up Circulation on Foot

As discussed in the introduction, the basic character of just-in-time production and circulation in Dongdaemun, various designs in small batch, involves numerous microscale actors who are connected through an outsourcing network rather than large-scale enterprises who organize flexible production in a centralized system. While small scale, the retailers and wholesalers put on pressure for the sped-up production and would make the most profit out of the marketplace. Yet, as seen in Chanhee's or Murasaki's case, they also in many cases do not have a privileged position in the broader economy. The marketplace is also full of them, conducting intense labor to keep with the sped-up circulation of clothes.

Customers for wholesale markets have long been Korean and foreign buyers who hand carry their packages for their own retail business. As briefly mentioned in the introduction, frequent buyers from China, Central Asia, and Russia have formed ethnic business clusters around Dongdaemun. It was also a common practice for young Korean people who dream about opening their own store to spend many hours walking around and observing others' trades. If the retail malls brought a revitalization at the end of 1999, what sustained the demand for the domestic market in the 2000s was online space. While the off-line retail stores in the city did not radically expand, the proliferation of online shopping malls brought numerous individuals and microscale businesses. Some exceptionally successful stories—like Yejin Kim, who became famous with her nick name Saeoksonyeo (meaning, "four hundred million girl," because she made four hundred million won [about four hundred thousand dollars])—inspired more people to come to the marketplace.[10] Many of these entrepreneurs engaged in a trial period in which they commuted to Dongdaemun after their regular job during the day to watch people and clothes and to learn as much as possible about the operations of the wholesale and retail clothing industry. The hype surrounding online start-ups has escalated because of the relative ease with which prospective entrepreneurs can access the garment and fashion industry. As of 2018, it is possible to launch an online shopping mall, stand-alone website, or a personal blog, with start-up funds of five million won (approximately five thousand dollars). Many online entrepreneurs use limited space and work mobile, mostly starting their clothing retail business in their home without renting any office or store space. A 2015 study showed that e-commerce in South Korea occupied 3.4 points of GDP and 14.2 percent of retail sales, and it has been increasing (G. Kim, 2015). Clothes are the major purchase item for young people, accounting for about 40 percent of sales at online shopping malls, partly because of the presence of Dongdaemun's wholesale sector in the heart of the city.[11]

The online retail business and socialization brought more people to the in-person wholesale market, including those who were seeking more competitive products for their online stores, creating a particular version of "flexible" commodity circulation. State, corporate, and individual agents sponsor publications, informational websites, and workshops to guide entrepreneurs in how to launch a business. Most importantly, people learn that they must immerse themselves in Dongdaemun market well before they open their own store, ask questions of the merchants and designers, and learn the lay of the land by walking around as much as possible. At the same time, while the new virtual market made Dongdaemun more financially viable and physically dense, it renders the economic and social disparity more visible than in the past. Research shows and news media report that e-commerce hype has been intensified with increasing unemployment and unstable employment. However, nearly 80 percent of newly launched online stores fail and close. The media exposure of the exceptionally successful cases of celebrity CEOs contributes to this hype.

The virtual market connects Asian cities in interesting ways. One Japanese buyer I met in Dongdaemun market, Tanabe, was about to launch an online shopping mall after several years of trading apparel between Vietnam and Japan. He said that good clothes (which he perceived as functional features and trendy designs) are no longer enough for the small-scale online shopping malls to survive in competition with major apparel companies and other emerging online malls. Instead, he said, he needs to develop "stories" for each of the products he sells. During the interview, Tanabe described these stories as composed of integrated textual and visual themes, the coordination of different clothes, and the development of a sense of atmosphere. Compared to manufacturers in Japan, Tanabe felt that Dongdaemun responds quickly to global fashion trends, and he felt inspired by the customers there to develop his stories. Unlike the small city where he lives in Japan, in Dongdaemun Tanabe was able to observe huge crowds moving around clothes, including wholesale buyers, designers, young customers who are running online shopping malls, or unknown passengers, while he ordered clothes and designed the concept for his own online shop. In this way, Tanabe became familiar with the wholesalers' peculiar processes of consumption, design, and production, developing unexpectedly close relationships with the salespeople in the process. Through these interactions, the fashion trends, transaction skills, and pricing in Dongdaemun become visible to buyers like Tanabe. Without knowing any Korean or utilizing any sort of mediation, he has still developed the necessary knowledge for his business by watching, imitating, and mingling with others as they interact with clothes and each other.

Dongdaemun market's location in the heart of the city is linked with the 24-hour operation of various retailers and allows them to be loosely connected to garment work and make it into a personal project. When I first met Somi in 2012, she was taking a semester off from a graduate school to work as a full-time library intern to prepare her master's thesis in library science. On top of her internship at the library, Somi also tutored an elementary school boy and ran an online shopping mall with her friend. Sohee's daily life was packed. Immediately on waking up, Somi would check her phone for the orders that she received after she went to bed and head out to Dongdaemun. By 8 a.m., Somi finishes buying the shoes ordered during the night in the shoe wholesale market. She then rushes off to arrive at the library for her internship by 9:30 a.m., and on the way she stops at a 24-hour convenience store to send the shoes to the customers and pick up breakfast. While she works, her smartphone stays on silent but constantly flashes notifications of incoming orders. Somi ends her workday at the library at 6:30 p.m., and then off she goes to tutoring an elementary school student. After having finished her class or other chores, Somi heads to Dongdaemun around 9 p.m. to pick up clothes on order and to find more items to post on her blogs. On the way back home, Sohee stops at the 24-hour convenience store again to ship off the clothes she bought.

Young people like Somi, who are in a precarious economic situation, must seek opportunities beyond their regular jobs. For these young entrepreneurs, Dongdaemun's nighttime has inspired many clothes lovers to take a second job or explore new work. In two years, Sohee's online store became somewhat stable as her retail items filled a niche in a market for short-length clothes. Her customers liked her clothes because they are different from generic "petit" sizes and cater to a body type that is, in their words, "short and round." On her blog, Somi, her readers, and her customers chat about their shared experiences of finding clothes with a right "fit" for their body type and tips to coordinate the items that are sold. In one interview, Sohee described the motivation that she has for her work, saying,

> I have not meticulously calculated all the costs [that go into a business like this] like bus fare, the snacks I often buy on the way, or my own labor walking and running every day. I just learned that it is good to make a 30 percent profit and added 30 percent to the price of the items that I sell. I did not make tons of money but . . . cultivated my own fashion in the way that I would not have done if I was hanging out only with my graduate school classmates. It makes my life fuller, and I learned a lot.

Somi attended a government-sponsored program for online commerce and learned about pricing, tax registration, and legal requirements. The "30 percent profit margin" is a piece of basic knowledge that she learned as business management and applied to her store. While not systematically calculated, it has been working OK in the way she runs this business without any warehouse, office, or stock of clothes.

As such, the time-space of the fast fashion circulation that she materializes through her blog is extremely short cycled, small scale, and informal, intimately tied with her own walking and working trajectories in this city. Somi was proud of her most successful item over the last two years, a "gel flat" (*jel peullet*), women's flat-heel shoes made of malleable soft rubber with an open toe, which were highly convenient for the rainy season in the summer. She found the shoes in a wholesale store of Dongdaemun, tucked in an alley that would not be easily found. With the wholesaler of this hidden gem, she has developed a good relationship and made the shoes as a steady item for three years. As always, Somi only bought three pairs— one for herself, two with different colors to use as samples. The shoe wholesaler never thought that young women would like the design, but it turned out to be a big hit when her blog sold out before she could fill 120 orders. As a result, Somi had to go around the market to find similar shoes to fill the backlog.

Somi's day comprises multiple cycles constantly in motion, layered within and around a nine-to-six workday. The fast pace of commodity circulation is possible thanks to the digital technologies and media that make online monetary transactions, high-end smartphones, and individual blogs an easily accessible personal and commercial space. At the same time, it involves various subjects' quick and multiple visits to Dongdaemun and face-to-face interactions in their tightly packaged daily routine. The landscape of fashion—and those who embodied and populated it—creates a material scene that people experience and imagine through their entrepreneurial desires and trials.

Temporalizing Space

The Dongdaemun Division of the famous Yeoido Full Gospel Church actively incorporated the nighttime working schedules of the vendors. Buried in the wholesale mall buildings, the church held collective *saebyeok gido*, or "predawn prayers," every day, which is thought to symbolize the devoutness of its members. While often translated as "dawn prayers," the Korean word *saebyeok* is less "eventful" than "dawn" as it refers to the time when the east sky gets lighter, typically after midnight and before sunrise. In the church's 2012 newsletter that illustrated the success of predawn prayer, the pastor of the Dongdaemun Division wrote: "In Dongdaemun, tenants [of the shopping malls] are required to be present during business hours, until 6 a.m. [They] could get charged penalties and eventually get evicted if they leave their store vacant or close multiple times during business hours. It means that the attendees of our predawn prayers made tremendous effort despite this risky condition and proves their remarkable spiritual devotion."[12] The main pastor of the church leads the predawn prayers that start at 5:00 a.m. every day. One or two hours before the predawn prayers, the pastor goes around the wholesale market stores to meet his churchgoers and others to pray for the individuals and encourage them to come to the collective prayers that will be held starting soon. Most of the church members are wholesalers and traders, and the pastor accommodates their work conditions and schedules. A few months earlier, the church even proudly announced that it would be "open" all day long, for all members from any Christian denominators and all nationals who visit Korea, allowing for the particular time structure of Dongdaemun and celebrating the thriving market.

The commercial success of the market agents is incorporated as an essential part of collective prayer cycles and events, such as Consecration Congregation for New Spring Collection (*bom sinsangpum chukbokseonghoe*), typically in March, or the foreign language programs for the vendors.[13] Through these practices, the prayers become a mundane ritual, and go in hand with the commodity cycle in the marketplace. These religious practices merge the dusk and the dawn for the workers and forge the lived temporality of the devotees, who need to make a deliberate effort to accommodate the prayer into their tight marketplace schedules. The material and affective energy of being awake to work, make money, and pray together saturate the dawnscape for the Christians in Dongdaemun.

This blatant articulation of spiritual piety and economic prosperity is embedded in the context of South Korean evangelical churches and their recent practices. Originally, dawn prayer would emphasize an individual practice and meditation. Numerous references in the Bible suggest the dawn is the time when people are spiritually serene, not disturbed by the complex chores of life yet. And these features make it optimal for making the most direct connections with God. Daebok Choi (2012, 163–64), a Christian pastor and the author of *Saebyeoge Moksumeul Geolda* (Betting your life on the dawn), suggests finding a way to attract Christian youth to the predawn prayers: "These days we have a lot of 24-hour businesses prospering around us. . . . On my way to church for predawn prayers, even in that early time, I see many people coming out of drinking or *noraebang* [karaoke] stop by the 24-hour convenience stores. These places are more prosperous than I would expect. Today we are living in a world where predawn businesses flourish. . . . I thought, if a convenience store gets that crowded with the energetic young people, then why not our dawn prayer meetings?" According to Choi, the most frequent attendants of predawn prayer typically have been housewives and elderly people, whereas young Koreans, especially men, are key players in the expanding nighttime economies and would be more resistant to making their way to church that early in the morning. Choi's hopeful (and quite gendered) projection is that to redirect the energy of young people and men to the dawn prayers would require greater commitment and discipline but would be worthwhile. A dawn prayer meeting populated with young people would render the future of the Christian church potentially able to "transform the world in its midst" (Choi 2012, 165).

As in Choi's observation, the temporal qualities of the 24-hour city—the dawn and the youth—are tied to both capitalist and Christian yearnings for growth and fulfillment and create the particular spaces of the church and the city. Indeed, 24-hour businesses have been thriving in Seoul—not only cafés, movie theaters, shopping malls, saunas, and hair salons but also numerous *hagwon* (private tutoring classes) for foreign languages, gyms, and churches. Populated twenty-four hours a day, they create an environment for young people to stay awake, maximizing their time by engaging with more "productive" activities in public, either by spending money for leisure or by disciplining oneself mentally, bodily, or spiritually. Predawn prayer has been a quintessential aspect of Korean evangelism[14] since the very beginning of Christianity in Korea that churches promote internationally.[15] While some criticize the religious institution's developmental ideologies that aim for a rapid growth through dawn prayers, others associate the dawn prayer with a new mode of life in neoliberal Korean society where time manage-ment is a virtue.[16] It is not rare to see Christian self-help publications frame time-management tips as a lesson from the Bible. These publications actively draw from "an early bird" discourse and secular prosperity and are expressed with Christian values. Many also tell success stories of well-known profession-als and celebrity figures who have actively incorporated dawn prayers in their lives and eventually experienced "miraculous" transformations of their lives.[17] As Dongjin Seo (2009, 310) argues, there is no salient difference between the secular, spiritual, and market-driven self-development in that they all delineate an entre-preneurial self.[18]

However, what we can see from the collective ritual of predawn prayers is more than its convergence with individualized piety and neoliberal self-management. The prayers materialize religious aspiration for spiritual life in a way that parallels temporalize the nightscape (or dawnscape) of Dongdaemun. The urban density, transportation, and built environment seem to condition the scale of the dawn praying meetings. In turn, the material and affective energy coming from the inter-mittent and regular meetings shape the one segment of the 24-hour city space. Ethnographic work by religious studies scholars highlights the way that public ex-pressions and practices of piety fabricate the urban texture. Lara Deeb's (2006) analysis of Shi'i Lebanon suggests that an intricate urban texture consists of sights, sounds, and temporal cycles. As much as the visible presence of images, built forms, and people traffic, the invisible atmosphere configure and compose the space and embodied experiences of the city. This is temporalized space, inter-woven with the rhythms of the city and subjective senses of time.

Conclusion

This opening chapter has traced the ways in which Dongdaemun's nighttime has become populated and animated. The micropractices constantly create the energy and affect that imbues value in both the commodities and the space. While the no-tion of abstract time assumes that the daily cycle of economic activities is being stretched out or extended through the night and that the fast pace of productivity dictates all aspects of peoples' lives, this chapter has shown how fast-fashion mate-rially, affectively, and virtually connects local and transnational cities, as well as differently positioned people in the marketplace. This cycle of work, life, and en-ergy is also appropriated and reinvigorated by religiously accentuated time.

The "24-hour" aspect of this marketplace is tightly connected with those who may or may not be present in the place at the moment: those who materialize the "flexible" and "just-in-time" production and circulation in small scale, on foot and in hand, while forming a huge crowd of the night. Seamstresses like Sinhye, whom we met in the opening section of this chapter, manufacture the physical material to be sold in the market and engage the marketplace itself to draw from its energy (and consume the space itself, in a way). And in doing so, they in turn form the crowd that animates others. Subsequent chapters focus on workers who are involved in various stages of garment making. As I discuss in those chapters, people also move between domains of designing, manufacturing, wholesaling, or retailing, through their own occupation or their familial ties. The commodities and workers materially, physically, and affectively tie the daytime and nighttime and experience it as a continuum rather than as a division.

The routinized intensity—the dissident rhythms, tempos, and cycles of the everyday practices and dense footsteps of those who conduct immensely tight schedule of the day—both vitalizes the city and ultimately creates this temporalized space. As I will continue to show in the following chapters, delving into the work of Korean manufacturing workers, designers, and traders, the temporal-spatial fabric of the nighttime space is connected to intricate garment design, manufacturing, and selling networks brought to fruition by the work of individual agents who merge with the crowd, whose working hours are all different, and whose role is not apparent, sometimes hidden and imitated, and also multiple. Their physical presence is constitutive of the space, the affective atmosphere from their interactions and practices, and their intentional and unintentional performance of the vitality, meanings, and signs of the 24-hour city.

INTIMATE NETWORKS

Misun was a fifty-six-year-old seamstress with almost thirty-eight years of experience sewing in the Dongdaemun market. I first met her one evening at MANI, a labor nonprofit and social enterprise where I was volunteering as part of my research. Misun was attending a dinner event there, and I asked her if she was willing to be interviewed. When I started my fieldwork in Dongdaemun in 2006, I was told over and over that without having a personal network, it would be nearly impossible to interview workers or access garment factories. Many people from the wholesale markets and government offices warned me that the garment factories are hidden and hostile to strangers as they often had not formally registered as a business body. While these admonitions initially made me nervous to approach the factories, once I got to know factory workers, these worries would turn out to be unfounded. Many workers, like Misun, were quite forthcoming in discussing their work and life with me. For example, in addition to her being a seamstress in a garment factory, one of the first things I learned about Misun was how proud she was of raising her daughters on her own after her divorce while managing her female-only household. She invited me to her factory, which she described as being "on the second floor, two doors down from the biggest button store on the street." There was neither a signboard nor an address for the factory. When I finally found the obscure little place, nobody seemed the least bit perturbed as I began to work alongside Misun. The factory owner barely glanced at me, while the other ladies simply smiled and gladly took the juice that I had brought to share. Misun explained that it was common for family and friends to visit during work hours. As I sat with Misun and chatted, occasionally fetching her stacks of cloth or a roll of thread, nobody even skipped a beat.

Misun had once owned a factory, which she ran in her house. Back then, the second floor of the factory was reserved for the family, while the first floor was dedicated to the factory workshop. Her daily schedule was fluid as she moved between her sewing machine, her children, and the factory workers. As the head seamstress working out of her home, she could go up to see her children throughout the day. When I asked her why she had decided to move to this other factory, where she just rented a machine and set up for work, she brought up her divorce. Things had been fine between the couple while her husband worked in their home factory. Over the years, however, he became less diligent and was seldom present in the factory. "He was not working hard," Misun told me. "It was bad for the factory and bad for the family. So I kicked him out!"

I was surprised and asked, "Do you mean you kicked him out of the factory or out of the family?"

"Both," she replied, with an air of satisfaction, "I fired him!"

Misun's story illustrates how working people's personal lives and work trajectories intertwine within Dongdaemun market. As witnessed in Misun's exclamation that she "fired" her husband and thus proclaimed the simultaneous end of her marriage and their factory, the stories that I explore in this chapter reveal that personal and intimate relationships between spouses, family, and friends start, expand, or fall apart alongside the instrumental relationships in the market. Like Misun and her family business, manufacturing, wholesaling, and retailing sites and their workers are connected in messy ways. Working relationships are often forged through personal networks and family narratives, and the histories of the manufacturing scenes often overlap. Wherever there is a sewing machine in a home, there is a gongjang (factory). Marriage, family, friends, and work are thus often inextricable, as they drive and reproduce the speed of garment production and consumption that characterize the glitzy and glamorous downtown market that is only a few blocks away.

The intimate networks between married couples, parents and children, in-laws, siblings, friends, and colleagues were the integral foundation for the sped-up cycle of production and circulation as well as the survival of a labor force in proximity to the marketplace. As briefly explained in the introduction, after mass manufacturing declined in downtown Seoul, the networks have maintained the just-in-time supply chain of garment production and circulation within the spaces of factories and markets. By intimate networks, broadly speaking, I am referring to social relations that are physically and/or emotionally close, personal, romantic, private, caring, or loving (Constable 2009, 5). The nature of this relationship, however, is not necessarily supportive, loving, and enduring; rather, it often complicates the intricate supply chain that can be otherwise conceived as merely fragmented, instrumental, or utilitarian. More specifically, I emphasize their *mutual dependency and care*, where husbands, wives, daughters-in-law, friends, and coworkers often work together for a long time each day or for a long time over the course of their lives. Their understanding each other's work as well as giving attention to personal vulnerabilities and needs shapes the nature of their work and their relationships, or as the sociologist Viviana Zelizer (2005, 14–15) described it in her study on intimacy, "knowledge and attention that are not widely available by third person." These relationships evolve and expand together with the economic processes in Dongdaemun life, involving subtle gender negotiations, in such a way that intimacy and the market are coproduced and mobilize one another (Wilson 2004; Yanagisako 2002) in their own pursuit of rapid material production. The history of this urban economy is woven within the personal histories of the individuals whose skills and desires have simultaneously nurtured and sustained their intimate relationships and their work.

Women's work is a critical driving force for Dongdaemun's production and circulation, and it takes multiple forms. The value they produce is always much more than what they are compensated for in calculable, numeric returns within the frame of wage labor; and the times of their daily routine blur the boundary of work time. Feminist scholars have paid attention to how women's double duties complicate the analysis of work time[1] as their activities and relations are compounded in their homes, public spaces, and workplaces (Aitken and Carroll 2006; Ladner 2009; Odih 2003). This chapter pushes this insight to argue that women workers manage their multiple roles in reproducing the family and monetary value at the same time, rendering the intimacy as integral in the smooth and sped-up cycle of commodity production circulation. Stories like Misun's show that these kinds of mutually dependent and sometimes exploitative relationships produce, create, and sustain economic and intimate space together but carry the risk of breaking them apart at the same time. Like Misun's firing of her husband who does not satisfy her as a coworker or marriage partner, the ethnographic account that I draw from here highlights the subtle dynamics and tensions between what is intimate and what is economic and challenge the perceived division between notions of care and impersonal economic rationalities, without erasing or reconciling the differences between them. The intimate and instrumental relationships not only create the conditions to rise, evolve, and expand but also set limitations on and destroy one another. The division of labor in the factories and marketplaces are interwoven in the histories of family, and the temporal span and the meaning of the family's life span is connected to the past and future of factories and markets.

Home-Factories and Flexible Production

Changsin-dong, the neighborhood where Misun's factory is currently located, used to be a famous residential district for garment workers in the 1970s and 1980s. After the number of mass-manufacturing factories in adjacent Dongdaemun decreased in the late 1980s and 1990s, the neighborhood started to become populated by home-based outsourcing factories by those who had lost their jobs in large-scale factories. Technically these factories would be considered closer to home-based "workshops," indicating their smaller scale in comparison to typical "factories," which connote mass production and systemized assembly lines. However, Dongdaemun workers call their workplaces *gongjang* (factories), regardless of the small space and production capacity. Within Seoul's garment manufacturing factories, small-scale factories with one to four workers occupy 63.5 percent; ones with five to nine workers occupy 23.4 percent. Especially within the four northeast districts around Dongdaemun, where these garment manufacturing factories congregate, smaller factories with one to four workers reach to 72.4 percent (Korea Labor Institute 2012, 22). And I call these microbusinesses "home-factories" to mark their distinguishing social characteristics.

Most individuals who built and maintain their home-factories had been trained and worked in the mass-production factories in the 1970s and 1980s. Even during the export-centered manufacturing period, Dongdaemun factories hired their workers as *gaekgong*: contract workers who were technically self-employed, and they work either in their home or in the factory. The work patterns both undermined labor rights and led workers to develop the skills necessary to complete garments. The seamstresses typically worked with apprentice seamstresses. It took several years to move forward along the apprenticeship from entry-level stitching assistant (*bojo sida*) to assistant seamstress (*sida*), and then to master seamstress (*oya*). *Oya* means "parent" in Japanese, but it is also used for parent-like roles (managers, owners) in economic and social groups. *Sida* derives from the Japanese word *shita* meaning "underneath" or "underling."

Many master seamstresses were paid by the piece and shared a portion of their earnings with their apprentices. The faster they produced, the more they could work. This piecemeal gaekgong system made it impossible for garment workers to secure stable employment with benefits and insurance, as well as to claim legal protection. This was also the way in which workers developed a sense of independent micro entrepreneurship and craftsmanship, eventually taking charge of the whole process of garment making and becoming sewing masters. Misun, for example, took five years to advance down the career path of a seamstress and was very eager and quick to master each stage, partly because everything related to garment production fascinated her. Gradually, like the master seamstress whom she had apprenticed under, Misun began to dream about opening her own workshop. Once she became a master, she moved from one factory to another until she met and married a pattern maker.

Because the seamstresses had to share their pay with their assistants, long-term trust between the women became important. Sisterhood and friendship between seamstresses and assistants were frequent topics of conversation among my interviewees, and many seamstresses first entered the manufacturing scene through a family member's invitation to work as an assistant. By the time workers opened their own factories, many of them partnered with family members—sisters are the most preferred—so that incomes could combine to meet family needs. This sharing of incomes and responsibilities was even more prevalent within marriages. The gendered division of labor was such that many women took on the stitching work, while men did the fabric cutting or pattern making.[2] Cutting and stitching work are the basic components for operating a garment factory and are often found in the narratives of neighborhood marriages and families. It was not with the explicit purpose of making a collaborative unit for a factory that Misun married a fabric cutter; the aspirations of building up a family business and the desperation they shared about the dwindling garment manufacturing industry made their intimate and economic partnership natural. As her marriage followed the common pattern of other workers' marriages, Misun spoke about the typical nature of her marriage and life in the factory:

> You just spend so much time there, and you do not meet anybody else. Many people end up marrying someone who is doing the same job since you already know, as a couple, that you can make garments and keep the income in the family. You don't have any other resource than your own labor.[3] We were just people who believed in our skill and our bodies. Many of my colleagues intentionally looked for a partner [who did patterns] so they could work in the same way. And many marriage matches were already set up that way.

As wages rose in the late 1980s and early 1990s, large-scale factories left Seoul for cheaper labor costs in countries like Vietnam or Indonesia (Kim 1997). As a result, many garment workers began opening their own small factories by working at home in the neighborhood nearby the market or in very cheap rooms in a residence. Garment workers earned their living as either a partner in a married team or simply by setting up a sewing machine in one corner of their houses. These home-factories remained informal, without registering as a *saeopjang* (business site), even after they expanded beyond five workers, which was the legal threshold for formal registration.[4] The stories suggest not merely that these factories utilized the space of home but that the home and factory often formed and grew together. These small home-factories proliferated in the 1980s and 1990s when Dongdaemun's emerging retail malls required more flexible manufacturing supplies to keep up with the ever-changing fashion trends. Today, home-factories, residences, and stores are often mixed together, with few boundaries and distinctions marked within the built environment.

Indeed, it is very difficult to find these home-factories. As I experienced when wandering through the streets looking for Misun's description of the "largest button store on the block," in this area there are often no clear street signs. Even some of my interlocutors who had worked in home-factories found it difficult to point out the places where they had been previously employed. Later on, during my fieldwork, I developed some skill in recognizing these factories. For example, I found that steam vents on the sides of residences and industrial garbage bags stuffed with cloth scraps subtly marked home-factories (figure 2.2).

Signs and flyers recruiting workers for specialized units for outsourcing networks (figure 2.2) would also suggest the presence of nearby factories and laborers with particular skills. Along their network a commodity moves forward, shaping the daily cycle of the neighborhood. Pattern makers (*paeteon-sa*) and fabric cutters (*jaedan-sa*), or those who perform both tasks, are mostly men, but relatively high-paid jobs. Late at night or early in the morning, they produce paper patterns and cut the thick piles of cloth, according to piece, to be assembled and distributed to the stitching workers working in the factory or in their own houses. Stitching workers, mostly women, would occupy the biggest number and work during the day. Some workers are specialized in particular sewing machines such as overlocking (*oba-sa*), buttonhole making, or embroidering (*jasu-sa*). After initial stitching and assembling, clothes go through washing factories nearby in the evening. Washing factories for jeans and denim clothes, which requires chemical washing or physical destressing to create particular patterns and texture on the fabric, are commonly large scale, located outside Seoul, and often occupied by foreign migrant workers. Then, in finishing factories commonly called *siage* (a Japanese term for finishing or polishing), workers use heavy irons not only to smooth out the surface but to define lines, pleats, or shapes. Finishing factories sometimes hire *madome-sa* (from the Japanese term *matome*, meaning "wrapping up") to work in their factories or the person's own house. Madome-sa, typically women, do all kinds of hand work, including making decorative stitches, hand-stitched hems, and buttons for delicate fabrics, or removing loose threads and debris for final products. Their work also includes other miscellaneous jobs, such as connecting clothing tags with safety pins or making and attaching ribbons. Older women in their sixties to seventies, who are not trained in machine stitching or are retired seamstresses, are common groups in this occupation. The finished products are delivered to the wholesale market nearby, as described in chapter 1.

FIGURE 2.1. The streets of Changsin-dong. Residential buildings include home-factories. The signboard on the left bottom corner says, "Recruit: stitching person, *sida* [assistant], overlock stitching person."

Photo by the author.

The Japanese terms *oya*, *sida*, *siage*, and *madome* or other sewing terms combining English and Korean would sound unfamiliar to even ordinary Koreans and indicate the specialization and marginalization of the field. Despite the gradual change of the colloquial Korean language after the 1945 liberation from Japanese colonial rule and the government's postcolonial initiatives for Korean language

FIGURE 2.2. The streets of Changsin-dong. I could sometimes recognize factories by spotting these trash bags full of fabric parts.

Photo by the author.

purification (*gugeo sunhwa* or *gugeo jeonghwa*), Japanese terms are still frequently used in certain fields. The persistence of these terms in the jargon of garment manufacturing, metal tools and instrument manufacturing, or building construction, for example, indicate the socioeconomic marginalization of these fields. However, combined with Korean morpheme *-sa*, meaning "a person of a particular occupation," these terms indicate a distinct role that each person serves. Without highly structured mega factories in which one can expect a stable system of apprenticeship and training, one's own experiences, training, and understanding of one's own and others' works have become a more critical source.

Rapid industrialization prompted many individuals to become productive, to devote their time to learning and becoming adept at particular skills—the skills necessary for making garments and knitting families together. And these individuals' works are not coordinated by any centralized system. Many of them are connected as families, friends, or close neighbors, involving one another spontaneously or on a long-term basis. The intimate relationships of people and their knowledge, care, and codependence on one another has been integral as these different actors work together and drive the smooth sped-up production of the industry, amid the cycles of the everyday lives of family and commodity production, as well as the long-term development of networks. These informal microfactories in residential neighborhoods did not originate from a "traditional," preindustrial mode of craftsmanship but rather spurred off of the mass-manufacturing factories and spread out with functional and intimate networks, constituting the intricate supply chain of today. The transition involved more than an adjusted and rescaled mode of production. Many families and interlocutors I spoke with described it as an individual choice of how to pursue a life: what kind of dependence they formed in the decision and how the formal apprentice partnership of oya and sida became relocated to houses and drew on the language of sisterhood and friendship. As people reflected on their lives, they would also recount the transition from the standardized and centrally controlled production in the factories to the supply chain of subcontract units of garment manufacturing. From the vantage point of people's lives and relationships, history in Dongdaemun market does not always follow the evolutionary trajectory of the mode of production space shifting from the household economy to the industrial factory.

Rhythms and Cycles of Everyday Life

In home-factories, manufacturing work and relations rely on and reproduce an intimate network of couples, parents, children, and friends, where rhythms and cycles of everyday life are interwoven in the fast-paced production cycles. Jungyu and Hyeyeong's factory was one of the main venues where I got to meet with factory workers. Hyeyeong, a seamstress in her fifties, became involved in garment work for the first time when she married her husband, who had been a pattern maker in Dongdaemun. Her husband, Jungyu, was very skilled at making men's jeans. When he had mastered making men's pants, he decided to produce his own brand from a medium-sized factory they opened near Dongdaemun. I first got to know Jungyu through a neighborhood community event and then received permission to visit his factory. Eventually I got to know the stitching workers and fabric cutter of the factory, and I was regularly visiting twice a week and working as *sidaui sida*, meaning "assisting the assistant."

Ever since Hyeyeong and Jungyu got married, Hyeyeong has cooked and cared for their employees, whose numbers reached twenty-four at one point. At that time, she also worked in the overnight wholesale market, where she sold clothes that had been made in their home-factory. When they had to reduce the scale of their wholesale and manufacturing business, Hyeyeong opened a home-factory and focused her time there. Now she stitches with two other seamstresses and occasionally serves as a sida (assistant seamstress), helping them all day long. I often visited her home factory and assisted with menial tasks, such as snipping loose threads and folding tags for T-shirts. While there, I noticed that her husband would come into the factory only when he had a particular occasion to talk with the workers about things like paychecks. The rest of the time, Hyeyeong was in charge of the factory because she also worked on the manufacturing line.

Because the spatial boundaries between home and factory are porous, the meaning of work and relationships are hard to bound. While working in the home-factory, I often helped by collecting dirty lunch dishes and returning them to delivery restaurants. This was difficult to classify as a home or factory job because Hyeyeong and the other factory owners provided meals for their employees; having dinner on time was integral to completing the jeans and delivering them to the finishing line by midnight. One evening as I gathered dishes after a meal, Sunae, a skilled seamstress in the factory, told me not to return some dishes, as those dishes are *urigeo* (ours) and came from Hyeyeong's home kitchen on the second floor. Sunae seemed a bit hesitant in that moment as if she had realized that the word *urigeo*, used habitually by her, might sound confusing to an outsider. However, there was no alternative word, and I myself also became accustomed to the term; the boundary of "us" is not clear in this home-factory, where family and factory workers share extensive and intensive amounts of time together.

While the factory workers ordered food delivery, Hyeyeong would go up to the second floor to her own family's living space to prepare her family's meal. The typical delivery order consisted of rice, one main dish such as spicy tofu soup or grilled fish, and several side dishes like kimchi and vegetable pickles; but Hyeyeong often supplemented the food delivered to the workers with one or two homemade side dishes or a soup that she brought down from the second floor. To Hyeyeong, the mealtime seemed the moment when she was most aware of the fact that she was both at home and at the factory. For those in her own house, even if they were workers, she said that she needed to at least add a homemade dish. In Hyeyeong's everyday life, the boundaries of her own family and the workers were not clearly drawn. The home was right upstairs, and care, in the form of domestic labor (cooking), was being performed for coworkers in addition to her children and husband. To me, at first, it looked like a kind of double or triple shift combining the workplace and home, but Hyeyeong described her experience in somewhat different terms:

> I would forget about my own family if it weren't for the regular mealtime of the factory. Suddenly I realize that I am talking too fast and thinking too fast. I am stuck in the factory all day long, but [I know that] the workers in the factory feel that way too. The side dishes are nothing but a little bit of a distraction for myself, and for the other workers. . . . I used to

make twenty people food when we had just gotten married. We had twenty people in the house, including our son. That is how I started to work for the family and cook. It would feel weird to me if I make food only for my family.

For Hyeyeong, the meal was an example of this overlap between home and work, but the porous boundary and intimate dependency at work emerged frequently during my fieldwork. Earlier that day before she went to the grocery store to buy food for dinner, Hyeyeong borrowed money from Gija because she had run out of cash for groceries and the tutoring fee for her daughter. Gija heard Hyeyeong talking to her daughter on the phone, who called to remind her mother that the fee for the math tutoring class was due right after the factory's payday. It was a common happening and shared knowledge that, in the context of the small-scale supply chain of Dongdaemun, the payday of employees is the toughest day for the employers. Gija knew that Hyeyeong was running out of money, and she proactively offered to lend money to Hyeyeong. Moreover, Gija was the *oya eonni* (master seamstress and older sister) who had taught Hyeyeong how to sew and was leading the manufacturing line. Hyeyeong constantly consulted her about work and also about having to pause to work to prepare the family meal. The dinner budget for workers and the owner's family was communicated and managed within the work cycle of home-factory and family. Borrowing and lending cash was not a rare occurrence. Through constant chatting in person or on the phone or in social circles, manufacturing workers, especially women, got to know the lives and whereabouts of others in the factory and in the neighborhood. Through this kind of phatic labor (Elyachar 2010) that took place simultaneously during worktime, they get to know the needs of one another or others in the neighborhood, creating an informal infrastructure for channeling information, money, and care.

Many of my interlocutors had witnessed or utilized childcare on the workshop floor. Those who had the factory space in their own house often pointed out different corners where their (now grown-up) children used to eat or study. For those who worked at other factories in the neighborhood, it was not rare to see children coming in and out—to chat with the mother or get some pocket money on the way back from school. Even today, many seamstresses, either as gaekgong or on the assembly line, are constantly talking on the phone with their family and children by headset, while their hands are busy on the sewing machines or scissors. "I hardly had a chance to cook lunch or snacks for my children, but I made their clothes. I knew their bodies and the trendy style and fit, so they liked the clothes I custom made for them," Yujin, a seamstress said, who had been working in her own home-factories and others for more than thirty years. Yujin made extra pieces when she ran into a good design or good (and extra) fabric. Yujin emphasized the tactility of clothes for her care and affection: clothes are put on and cover one's body and carry her hands' warmth and love. She added, "It made me to feel that I am not an entirely bad mother." While not meeting the middle-class ideal of a stay-at-home mother, to "be always there" for children, garment workers' practices and narratives enabled "care" during their work time for commodity production.

By taking a "break" from the factory and going upstairs, Hyeyeong distinguished her home from the home-factory and herself as an employer distinct from the other employees with whom she spent at least twelve hours a day, six days a week. However, Hyeyeong's deliberate efforts to separate these spaces and keep her family and work time from being enmeshed were confounded by her contribution of domestic work to the factory below her home. Factory work—often stretching to 11 p.m. or later—became more arduous at night, when orders had to be finished on time and became more time sensitive. While Hyeyeong comes in and out during the day, it gets harder for her to leave in the middle of work at night. Leaving other people on the first floor to rest or to do house work, Hyeyeong said, made her feel uneasy. Involved in the home-factory as a duty to her family, Hyeyeong immersed herself in the factory, even more than her husband was; she shared and solved her own family's issues with her workers and wove the daily cycles together.

It is important to note that the family is not merely a functional foundation or social organization that smoothly buttresses the productivity of the factories. I extend the point that the anthropologist Sylvia Yanagisako (2002) made about the interrelated cycles and genealogies of capital and family. In her account of family firms in Italy, Yanagisako argues that family, kinship, gender, sentiment, and identity are coproductive with capital.[5] Companies' histories are interrelated with the life cycles of the families, suggesting that the family-business time span includes generational succession. I take her insight about intimacy, emotion, and sentiment and their relationship to capital yet push the point to further consider other complexities for the marginal people participating in the supply chain. That is, the reproduction of home-factories could get *stalled* because people put limits on their investments. When I asked Hyeyeong and Jungyu if they want to expand the scale of the factory for their children to inherit it, both said, no. Jungyu further explained why:

> We don't have much vision for continuing this. Look at the house. It's our house and the factory. Our lives have not changed at all, ever since we moved to Changsin-dong. What changes do you expect to see, when you see this never-changing neighborhood? We want them to do something different in college. They are a generation that would rather work

in fast food than in front of a sewing machine, no matter what they get paid. Many of us are working this hard because we do not want our kids to do this at all.

In Jungyu's case, the family-business time span prevented the succession. This refusal to expand the business or bequeath it to children was common in most cases, regardless of specific occupation in the garment industry, from gaekgong stitching workers, wage laborers, or owners of garment shops. Even though my interlocutors valued what they acquired in the factories and home-factories over time, they were also aware of the class distinction and the social perception of garment labor as being marginal. I asked what changes the couple had experienced while working in Dongdaemun and what they thought about the marketplace's transformation from mass-production factories to a touristy shopping district. Jungyu asked back, "What changes would you expect? Don't you see this place looking like thirty years ago?" Jungyu meant the shabby neighborhood and the unchanging marginalization of workers. I should note here, though, that Jungyu's factory has been relatively stable. Moreover, he once owned a wholesale store where he sold denim pants that he and his staff designed. As Jungyu once mentioned, with a bachelor's degree from a college in Seoul, his son might not earn as much in monthly income as Jungyu himself does. Jungyu's somewhat pessimistic sentiment related to the arduous working conditions and the fluctuation and instability of the market, and more to the general perception of contemporary South Korean society that devalues manufacturing labor. Jungyu hoped his son would not have to work in such a stigmatized industry. Like many other factory owners, designers, storeowners, and staff, Jungyu and Hyeyeong constantly made plans to leave the market and envisioned an end to having to spend time nurturing their business and home at the same time.

This family, like others in this area, which had formed, dwelled, and disbanded in the factory, has participated in and sustained this massive garment-market transformation for the past thirty years, while laboring to support the fast-fashion industry cycle that requires flexible textile manufacturing units. Squeezed into neighborhoods full of residential homes, the condition and the scale of factories have barely expanded. Similarly, the new demand of flexible production, the rising popularity of Dongdaemun as shopping and leisure space, and the embeddedness of working-class family histories have restricted the further development of the home-factories themselves. The expansion and extension of the home-factory business in this context involves more consideration of the spatial and intimate contours of people's visions of the future, for themselves and their children. Indeed, kinship is coproductive of capital; but for the same reason, the aspirations and desperation of families set limits on the perpetuation of capital and instrumental efficiency. For some families, the most successful factory business would never be handed down to children. Ideally, for Jungyu and Hyeyeong, the children would leave to do other things.

As such, intimate work relationships betray the intrinsic qualities of enduring, personal, and stable relationships, and home-factories are not necessarily a contained place for one integrated family. Rather, the presence of family members and married couples in home-factories carries complex meanings associated with aging bodies, accumulated sewing skills, and the uncertainties of the garment market. Sindang-dong, a district ten minutes' drive from Dongdaemun market, also accommodates home-factories in residential buildings slightly bigger than those of Changsin-dong. In Sindang-dong, the neighborhoods are better organized with taller buildings four to five stories high. Accordingly, the home-factories are larger in both size and capacity. Juhyeon, an assistant in her late fifties who worked at a factory here, said that she was the only employee whose spouse was not working at the same home-factory; all the other employees were married couples in which one worked as the master seamstress or as the tailor and the other worked as the assistant. I met Juhyeon through MANI's sewing advancement class. Juhyeon explained that she wanted to expedite the process of becoming a master seamstress by taking a class, as her partnership with her master seamstress was not as tight as that of married couples. These pairs are all gaekgong teams (self-employed workers paid by the piece), and each team works on different items ordered by different wholesalers. The home-factory owners operated as subcontractors, taking orders, procuring materials, and distributing materials and orders to these gaekgong teams, who will then be paid by the piece.

Among the other workers working as a team, Sanghui and her husband were from Hwaseong, a city on the outskirts of Seoul. Sanghui worked as a master seamstress, and Hosik was a cutter apprentice when they first met. Hosik did not become an independent pattern maker but learned the basic skills for running a home-factory. For a few years after they were married, they worked in a very small home-factory but soon moved out of Seoul. The couple worked various jobs in order to raise their children and settle down in Hwaseong. After the children grew up, the couple started to commute to Dongdaemun, knowing that there was work available, although life would be harsher because of the higher living cost of the city.

As a gaekgong team, Sanghui and Hosik worked in the factory that I visited. They spent almost all day in the home factory, from 9 a.m. to 10 p.m., or even later. They informed me that they have observed a lot of middle-aged or older couples who work and live in a similar way.

It's funny that we worked so hard in order to get out of here when we were young. But we are working like this again. . . . But at this age, it turns out this job is not that bad. Where else would I have this kind of thing? We always worked together when we were young, and [staying together all day long] is rather natural. As we got older, we realized that we did not have any plan for our later life. So we decided to go back to work. We do not talk much; we just work. You will know when you get older. But we made a good team, and we make a better income this way. Funny thing is that we don't even fight as much as before because we had to figure out a way not to.

Juhyeon added, "You guys are better off this way, since there are lot of *hwanghon ihon* [sunset divorce—divorces after the age of sixty or retirement], because when your husband retires, you are stuck with him at home! And you are even making money on top of it." After we all laughed, I asked Sanghui, "Did you intend it to be that way?" Sanghui replied, "Not really. We really needed money, as we have never had a job with benefits [for retirement]. But I did think about that and thought it wasn't actually a bad idea." Later she added, "The relationship at this point is different from what you, young people, would think." While the emphasis on the romantic and emotional connection weakened, the dependent partnership as a working unit brought a new kind of connection for the couple as they face their own aging. Their partnership has sustained this extremely arduous life of labor and also sustained the marriage in unexpected ways.

When the couple first moved to Dongdaemun to work again in the garment factory, they confronted a number of difficulties, and the relocation was not an easy process. At the beginning, the couple often stayed at 24-hour saunas around Dongdaemun and other factory neighborhoods until they got a cheap monthly rental unit. From the perspective of the couple's work, their residence as "home" did not differ much from the "home-factories" of Misun and Hyeyeong that I explored earlier in this chapter. This couple's marriage life in Dongdaemun is provisional, depending on the availability of jobs. Although their choice to work as partners again was an economic one, the meaning and the texture of intimate married life have changed through work, which has maintained the couple's stability and kept them together.

These workers' stories illustrate how their life courses, aging, and work cycles conjoin without an assumption of clear separation between intimacy and economy. Married couples' lives are shaped by their partnerships and made visible in the spaces of the home-factory, such that the presence of these relationships suggests shared histories in the garment sector and their training in garment-making skills. Juhyeon explained that couples in the home-factory, like the one she was working for, ensure that the home-factory is equipped with a stable, experienced pool of workers and that the products can be sold to the relatively upscale stores in Dongdaemun because of their quality.

The married relationship invokes each individual's embedded history and career in garment making: if both parties of the couple are working together, it often means that they began their careers in the mass-production period and have worked in the textile industry for decades. Moreover, if the husband was a master tailor, the couple's career would have started in the made-to-order tailoring business, even before the division of labor became common in the ready-made garment industry in the 1960s. The whole manufacturing scene currently faces the stigma of being a marginalized, obsolete sector, where the grueling labor is underpaid and undervalued. It is not only highly demanding to acquire advanced skills but also impossible to acknowledge one's skill in a formal certificate or standardized wage system. People told me that if I saw a home-factory with stable Korean couples working as teams, I could probably assume quality work and the home-factory's longtime experience and competitiveness in the market. The home-factory, then, is no longer merely a physical "container" of individual workers who happen to be family. Rather, the mobile, marginalized workers located inside the home-factory form and extend the reach of the home-factory, comprising the entangled time-space of both personal, intimate life and the home-factory.

Sisters and Families: Shifting Gender Divisions

Intimate networks in manufacturing, wholesaling, and retailing also go beyond marriages. In many home-factories as well as small-business wholesale and retail stores, family and friends work together. It is not rare to hear about the trajectories of people who used to work in wholesale markets or retail shopping malls and then moved to the manufacturing factories, or vice versa, as in the case of Sinhye (introduced in chapter 1). The familial networks facilitate these movements across manufacturing, wholesaling, and retailing and connections between small-scale factories and stores. The effort to maintain the sped-up cycle of production and circulations and extended work hours has brought more intimacy to the space of the market; it creates complex asymmetries and intersections between the domestic and public spheres, men's and women's work, and daytime and nighttime.

Miae and Jungi met in high school in Mokpo, a harbor town in southeastern South Korea. Jungi's sister first started a wholesale store in Dongdaemun market, and her business was going well. Inspired by his sister, Jungi began working as an independent salesman in Dongdaemun. A few years later, he and Miae decided to start their own wholesale store and get married. For the first several years, they spent most of their time in the market, selling clothes in the wholesale market at night and running around the garment material stores and outsourcing factories for manufacturing during the day. Now Jungi drops by the store only occasionally, while Miae works the night shift, from 8 p.m. to around 10 a.m. After their wholesale trading business wraps up, their designers work during the day and assist with some of Miae's work making orders for the textile material stores and garment factories.

After Miae and Jungi joined Jungi's sister in the marketplace, many other family members followed. For example, Miae's mother-in-law opened a store for men's pants in the same mall that houses Miae and Jungi's store. Across the hall, Miae's sister-in-law started a store selling women's jackets. Two years after I first met the couple, Miae's own younger sister, who Miae had left behind in her hometown many years ago, joined them and opened a store specializing in skirts. When I asked Miae if her family network had helped her business, I expected to hear about benefits from sharing information, networking market suppliers, or trading strategies. However, she asserted that it was more important for her to have her family's home-factories and businesses located in the same area because it allowed her to better develop and manage her family relationships. Ultimately, she could secure her own space of work from any interference from family obligation.

> We don't work particularly closely, and we don't necessarily favor each other over anybody else. . . . For women, in-laws are not comfortable, anyways. But they also understand my limits. My in-laws know that I am working here. I don't have to explain [when and how I work]. There are things that we understand about each other. We prefer not to bother each other. If they didn't work here, too, I would have had more family duties and stress. My friends with better jobs in companies have complicated lives; they never get enough rest as they take care of their own work during the day and have to do even more housework after their work time. Who would understand what they had to do during the day in their work?

For example, Miae did not feel pressure to take on family duties at holidays, such as New Year's Day or Chuseok (Harvest Festival). This is when Korean families traditionally gather and prepare food for their ancestors, an endeavor that typically exerts tremendous pressure on women's labor in the family. Miae's story is not merely a case of getting "excused" from her duties as a working mother. Rather, she serves the family not through her domestic labor, direct conversations, or holiday gatherings but through her work. In the wholesale malls, there are no walls or doors to close. In the small booth-like shops, working people are visible from the hallway, and the stack of clothes mark how well the store did that day. In passing her store or with one short greeting, Miae's in-laws would know how hard she was working at her business. Miae said they came to understand each other better—her mother-in-law and sister-in-law—than they did in the past. Even though Miae did not call them or dedicate her time to domestic chores, Miae said she felt that the harder she worked, the better she felt like she had filled in the gaps in the time they share as a family.

Therefore, the virtual connectivity and intimacy in time sustains and is fostered by the ceaseless productivity at night. Even though they work separately in different stores, they share their time, including the intense, endless round-the-clock work. This shared time makes for a different kind of "family time" that does not necessarily happen "at home." This intimacy connects women and spills over to the market, home, and home-factory. Further, these connections are not confined within the fixed boundaries of formal kinship. In Dongdaemun, all women, even customers, are called *eonni*, the Korean word for "older sister." The use of kinship terms is common, but the terms are more frequently used among women and reflect the informality of the interactions of the market.[6] Although it is common for customers and employers to call women engaged in service work eonni, the use of the term here illustrates the centrality of women in the garment industry with their relatively equal and intimate relationships that also stretch to extended female networks. Many of the women I encountered in Dongdaemun have had experiences working in apparel companies where the working relations are mediated by formal corporate structure and male-centered company outings to clubs and pubs after work. They compared their previous work to their current situation in Dongdaemun and often said that the long hours of nighttime work and the pressure to finish projects required more personal relationships and sensitivity. The frequent presence of real sisters and sisters-in-law sometimes complicates the meaning of *eonni* in the market and creates quasi-sisterhood among designers, sales staff, and vendors of various garment materials.

These dynamics of close relationships between women are different when the business also includes male owners. Jiyeong, a designer working for Miae and Jungi's store, found that the workload was divided in strange ways. She said, "The boss [Jungi] does not know much about our work. For us, he is just a guy who shows up twice a month and pays for things with the money that eonni [Miae] made. He drives a BMW and plays golf while eonni is working so hard!" Even though Miae and Jungi are both owners of their wholesale store, their experiences of work and time are very different. While Miae spends most of her time in the market with her cousin, sister, sister-in-law, and employees, Jungi spends most of his time with their children, his friends, or alone doing activities outside the marketplace. When I asked Miae whether she was upset about this, she said,

> There are so many divorces in this market. Did you know? Women here become really tough and support their own living. And they work at night. Many started off working together, but men usually cannot contribute that much to women's clothes. Rather than being stuck here at night with women, guys want to do some other business with the money their partners make and always end up failing. I have seen cases like that so many times, so I don't want to risk it. . . . He helps by not being here but still being a boss. I am helping my family by not being at home—I am not a very caring person.

The fact that Jungi is called "boss," the only nonkinship title in his wholesale store, shows that he and Miae do not share the same quality and meaning of time and interactions when it comes to their wholesale business. However, Miae needs her husband to maintain a physical and emotional distance from the market so that he does not interfere with her efficiency at work. Miae strategically treats her husband as a boss, allowing him to pay employees their salaries and to make important monthly transactions with their business partners, even though she does all the work and is respected as a boss in reality. Miae believes in her own ability to successfully run the business, so she treats him as a boss and gives him more leisure time in order to ensure that their home business runs properly and to secure his taking care of their children. Jungi becomes "the man" as "the head" of this family business, but not so much by a given structural position in the gendered hierarchy. Rather, this gendering process occurs because his detachment from the intimate ties that are integral to the market is necessary for the store's success, Miae's desire to work, and the family's needs at home.

The stories of garment home-factory workers suggest that a gendered division of labor persists in the marketplace yet is not static. This gendered division is constantly made and acted on by my informants in their efforts to cope with limited time, their desire to work, and the ways that they share time with colleagues and family. The familiarity, closeness, interlocutors, and emotional engagement with others—key features of the intimacy of this market—are often presented and experienced outside of bounded private and domestic space. The gendered divisions in these stories speak to particular articulations of exclusion and inclusion, marginalization and empowerment, and public and private spheres of work. These are the unsettled borders of families and a market on the move, despite the constant working hours and pressure of instantaneous, tailor-made production and circulation.

Conclusion

The stories presented above illustrate the various aspects of intimate and economic relationships between people in the fast-paced and rapidly transforming Dongdaemun marketplace. In focusing on the intimacy present in material production, it is possible to see how family residences, home-factories, and the market are not only physically and socially proximate but also coproductive rather than separate social domains. The space is interwoven with tight relationships in which people, especially women, play multiple roles to take care of others and keep those relationships integral. The nature of these relationships is caring, mutually dependent, and sometimes exploitative as they exchange and rely on one another's knowledge, skill, labor, and deep attention. This chapter has argued that these relationships have enabled the particular development of flexible and sped-up production and circulation in the context of the Dongdaemun area.

Feminist critiques have problematized theories of the evolution of capitalism that overemphasize the creation of a spatial separation between the domestic and public spheres as well as of the home and the space of production.[7] According to these critiques, macroview classical theories considered these spaces to not only have been separated but also hierarchically arranged in a sequential order with an economic shift from households to mass-production factories and then to financial markets and consumption spaces.[8] This assumption often makes the presence of the intimate domain in the market seem inadequate, obsolete, and thus undervalued.

The proponents and critics of round-the-clock production today share similar assumptions about intimate relationships as being the basic social unit in the market, which is both separated from and precedes the market. First, it is widely noted that the particularities of rapid production in Dongdaemun market depend on the prevalence of personal and intimate relationships spread throughout the market. On this, current observers have pointed out that the market's unique and personalized communications supplement the lack of a centralized business and a formally systemized supply chain (Kim and Shin 2000). Social ties, such as married couples and friends and family, organically connect manufacturing to the evolving market and contribute to the fast-paced decision making and flexibility needed to meet consumer demands. As Gerald Creed (2000) noted, social scientists often analyze social arrangements, in particular families, as what have facilitated and enabled the transitions of late-stage capitalism.[9]

Second, from the perspective of historical labor activism, it is this personal informality that serves as the exploitative apparatus and interferes with collective action and legal protections. Many former activists with whom I spoke lamented the loss of solidarity and collective action among laborers in the textile and garment

manufacturing industries due to the current family-centeredness and individu-
alism found in small home businesses. Similarly, studies of home-based, subcontracted factories highlight women's labor marginalization by linking the
cultural categories of "private" and "women's space."[10] The convergence of family
and factory is often analyzed through the ways in which quasi-family relationships frame mass-production factory relationships, drawing on the hierarchical,
gendered division of labor and the effective control of female workers (Ong 2010)
especially during the transition when industrial textile production dissolved and
transformed into numerous small home businesses. Small manufacturing sites
have received less attention as they moved into homes and converged with emerging shopping and tourism sectors.

From both perspectives on the family discussed above—as a functional, stable
system of efficiency or as a site of labor exploitation that materializes the market's
speed—intimate relations in the market are regarded as primary and naturalized
social units that precede the economy. However, both views have problems:
the functional explanation neglects the tensions and intensity that people have
to bear to materialize the imperatives of production speed; and the latter simpli-
fies the complex layers of relationships, motivations, and desires that people
have accumulated and invested in throughout their lives. Both posit family as
what is supposed to be before or outside the accelerated and evolutionary process of industrial capitalism and the modernization of South Korea.

Attention to the time and paces of everyday lives and the temporal narratives
of workers' lives reveal the more complicated features of the intimate spaces
therein and their significance in capitalist production and circulation. Contrary
to much of the evolutionary history of industrialization that depicts residences,
home-factories, and the market as the stuff of linear trajectories, intimate networks
have conditioned the way in which mass manufacturing and the flexible production sustained in the urban core of Seoul, without a clear disjuncture or dislocation
both in space and time. The overlapping life and work narratives in this chapter show how people invest their skills, money, and personal relationships over
the course of their lives. Many people who had invested their lives in mass factories in their youth later began home-factories and chose to keep the scale of their
work within the scope of their family, their residence, and their own workplace.
The stories in this chapter also highlight continuities that complicate the generalized perceptions of the South Korean urban landscape, which, at a glance, are
charged with the ruptures and rapid transformations of postwar modern history. As the garment industry speaks evocatively to "global restructuring" in industrializing societies, there is a strong expectation that manufacturing sites will
shift from the core to the periphery in the unequal world system of marginalized
labor and the logics of production cost (Bonacich 1994, 1–18). I argue that intimate

time-space is integral for better understanding the conditions and composition of life that have enabled and revitalized garmet production in the contemporary urban economy and the city's 24-hourization.

The ways in which my interlocutors create intimate relationships are deeply related to their subjective experiences and interpretations of time. The struggle over time necessarily unfolds in both work and intimate relations. The way time is spent at home and at work allows for the simultaneous circulation of garments and the forging of intimacy. Committed to their busy working schedules, the people I spoke with narrated how they think about their siblings, in-laws, spouses, and colleagues and how these relationships build trust, friendship, compassion, and partnerships. Individuals get involved in the industry in Dongdaemun, partaking in and extending these relationships, through which they also move across domains of manufacturing, wholesaling, or retailing and the spaces of home, factories, and marketplace. The dependency and care in these relationships shape the intricate supply chain of just-in-time production, interweaving the time for work and the time they share with others.

PASSIONATE IMITATION

Having worked in Dongdaemun as a contract buyer for retail stores in Seoul and then as a wholesale shop owner for twenty years, Eunae had developed a chronic dry-eye syndrome from her prolonged, irregular sleeping schedule and constant exposure to cloth dust. One of the results of this syndrome was that her eyes constantly watered. Whenever I talked to her, I could see this uncontrollable tearing up, something that worsened in the daylight. Wiping the corner of her eyes, she answered my questions about what it was like to run her business. I was expecting her to talk about her hardship and experience working at night, but Eunae spoke about her life as a creator of clothes. Specifically, Eunae shared the thrill she felt in being a part of quickly changing fashion trends, working closely with other hardworking people, partaking in the production and exchange of clothes, and how all of these experiences inspired her pleasure in design. Eunae explained:

> This is certainly better than the department store clothes. Sometimes I get inspired by trendy [designer] clothes, but I do make them better by adding and revising the pattern. I revise samples, repeating these five or six times until I am satisfied. . . . After all this, the design only gets better and more unique. Without my passion for clothes, I would have not continued this. . . . Those who are working here like clothes so much and have *passion* in their work. Otherwise, who would put up with this kind of life?

Eunae's comment implicitly responds to a common critique of Dongdaemun that casts the marketplace as merely a location for the sped-up repetition and replication of major designer clothes. Eunae seemed a bit embarrassed by describing her interest in her work as a passion. Jokingly, she asked me, "*Neukkihae* [Was that cheesy]?" This question reveals that she is conscious about the prevalent negative perspective on the design work done in Dongdaemun and the way the wider fast-fashion industry has been understood. Eunae and others did not claim their work was entirely original; however, they resisted the dominant view of their work as being mere imitations.

The word "passion" stood out in our conversations and appeared quite often during my fieldwork as an expression people used to highlight their feelings of dedication and care in contrast with the negative assumptions about the speed of Dongdaemun. This passion is not free of cost—I frequently observed the spontaneous tear, indicative of my interlocutors' long hours of work and exposure to light and cloth dust, regardless of their occupation. Yet the fatigue brought on by extended productivity and fast-paced work certainly coexists with and does not contradict the sense of attachment, intimacy, and motivation that my interlocutors have with their work. The use of the term "passion" was in stark contrast to the widespread perception of the design work of Dongdaemun's fast fashion or of third-world countries in general as mere replication of upscale designer clothes; and of manufacturing work as dull, boring, and endlessly repetitive. This chapter will first discuss how "imitation" has been constructed in the global and local context. Then, it will focus on two groups—designers and garment stitching workers (seamstresses)—to analyze how their narratives of care and attachment unfold onto and against the ideological underpinnings of the dichotomous division between creative and imitative work.

The Oxymoron of Passionate Imitation

Why might we expect "passionate" to be an inappropriate adjective to describe the work done in a place like Dongdaemun? At the core of this question lies the perception of the global division between imitation and creativity. As I discuss below, the intersection of the global reconstruction of the division of labor in the garment industry, the moral condemnation of fast fashion, and the rise of the knowledge/creative economy would require that we adjust the rigid, hegemonic frame for what can be considered creative. As a result, what does not fit into the narrow definition of creative work forms a broad and vague externality, a loosely bounded space of imitation, replication, repetition, or unbranded creation.

The international division of labor since 1960 has constituted a hierarchical structure that divides the site of design from the site of manufacturing (Bonacich 1994); and this structure evolved to posit the former as a site of authorized creativity. South Korea has taken part strategically in producing outsourced orders for apparel companies in Europe and North America. Branding and marketing in the apparel industry has intensified since the 1990s to the degree that some brand companies do not even have a single factory in their country of origin (Klein 2000). The critical portion of knowledge, design, and technology all come from first-world companies, which third-world manufacturing sites must follow or imitate. The proliferation of knock-offs of high-end brands in Asia since the 1990s has duplicated this historically constructed division of labor and reproduced the material and symbolic hierarchy of the West, which Hsia-hung Chang (2004) terms "glogocentrism." According to Chang, the overwhelming economic influence of globalization accelerated the rapid change not only of branded commodities but also, simultaneously, of counterfeit products. The reactive efforts to concretize the privilege and authorized trademarks of designer brands have contributed to the rigid definition of "creation" that presupposes spatial and temporal estrangement from other kinds of production practices, including those of "fake" goods.

The moral condemnation of the fast-fashion industry has also spread since the 2000s. Global fast-fashion brands, such as Zara or H&M, are known for the pace with which they deliver new items to their stores, reducing the time it typically takes retailers to move between initial sale and replenishment—from months to twice a week. Dongdaemun's even faster, small-scale production is not excluded from such criticism: each store puts out three to four new designs per day, and Dongdaemun as a whole produces hundreds of thousands. The quick turnover of merchandise forces people to work fast to meet the fleeting, ephemeral, and endlessly diverse desires and tastes that drive the market's trends. As briefly touched on in the introduction, such fast turnover of merchandise does not leave time for "good design" or good quality work. The negative conception of fast-fashion has intensified due to the multiple lawsuits filed against the global fast fashion brands concerning their unauthorized use of trademarks and design elements, as well as media reports on the conditions of these companies' manufacturing sites.[1] These incidents left the discursive rendition of fast-fashion designs and outsourced production as purely uncreative replications of designs and underpaid, repetitive-mind-numbing manufacturing labor, However, the "ethical" concerns were not only related to material and social relations but also to the hierarchy of brands, as Annamma Joy and her colleagues (2009) have addressed, where fast fashion is conceived of as unethical in contrast to luxury brands, which consumers view as ethical. In this zone of fast production and circulation, creativity, morality, respect, and love for garment making are assumed to be sacrificed for speedy returns.

The rise of discourse concerning creative economy solidified the narrow boundary of creative work, relegating most labor that does not fit this narrow boundary to the indistinct zone outside of it, which can never be creative, much less passionate.

The policy discourse in the 1990s in European metropolitan centers such as London or Milan, former industrial hubs, emphasized the increasing creative economy—such as the fashion design, media, and advertisement industries—as a vehicle for urban revitalization. This discourse posited the middle-class "knowledge workers in the creative economy" as exemplary figures who would lead the future economy (Pratt 2008). According to such discourse, the creative economy would generate not only economic growth; but also social and cultural inclusion and democratic and humanistic qualities (Arvidsson, Malossi, and Naro 2010). The transition from the material production of garments to the immaterial production of design, marketing and cultural events, and communication gave rise to the "creative class." The framing of creative work as fun, self-driven, and passionate, however, is not natural or neutral, as it justifies that industry's underpaid and arduous labor conditions. Numerous labor scholars saw the passion of workers and the discourse of passion lead to their own precarity (Arvidsson, Malossi, and Naro 2020; Pratt 2008) and reproduce the traditional notion of gender division at work (McRobbie 2018). Yet, the scope of this work focused within the cultural industries and did not question the very category of "creative work," reinforcing the rigid conjunction of creative work and passionate work.

East Asian states, as so-called latecomers to the rising creative economy, saw a pressing need to *expedite* the advancement of the creative economy. As Thomas Osborne (2003) points out, the prevailing ethos of "creativity" works, particularly in economic planning, as an ideology that is valued as a form of investment that enables a society to get "to the future first." In the 2000s, East Asian states desired this kind of transition and imposed great importance on the "creative economy" as a way of boosting national economies and urban revitalization (Currid 2007; Evans 2009; and Pang 2012). According to Laikwan Pang (2012, 9), the Chinese government's plan for "creative cities" is a response to critics who have characterized the country's creative economy as "slow" and to the widespread perception of China as a producer of fake goods. For former or current manufacturing sites, creativity, in the form of high-level labor, has been regarded as the necessary engine to drive these economies to the next stage in the hierarchical structure of global capitalism. As the mayor of Seoul in 2008, Sehoon Oh, declared, "We will have *design* to feed us." Creativity was very much regarded as a vehicle for economic development, just as labor-intensive manufacturing had functioned in the economic planning of the 1960s to the 1980s.

The South Korean state identified mindless "imitation" in Dongdaemun as one of the major culprits for the proliferation of fake goods in Korea and, more importantly, the lack of Korean-born brand names. In response, the government executed a five-year plan to develop a "future creative economy," assigning Dongdaemun's apparel production as one of its target sectors. As part of this plan, the state and city governments frequently cracked down on counterfeit items and sponsored research-and-development projects to normalize design practices and promote intellectual property. In 2008, the Ministry of the Knowledge Economy[2] launched several initiatives for "incubating" young designers and entrepreneurs in Dongdaemun, with the idea that these "key figures" would guide the future of the market by building up copyrighted and trademarked products.[3] Many other plans followed: the Seoul Fashion Creative Studio, for incubating workshops for designers, launched as a part of the wholesale marketplace in 2010; the Dongdaemun Fashion Business Center, to integrate designing and manufacturing actors in one location, opened in 2012; and the Dongdaemun Design Plaza, opened in 2011, also served as a physical presence to promote the idea (as I discuss in more detail in chapter 5).

In an effort to intervene in this context, MANI designed a project to promote more humane working conditions for the manufacturing workers, such as slower-paced, more creative fabrication processes. Though their foci are different, both projects—that of MANI and the state's plans—imagined "proper producers" with key creative capacities to expedite the market's radical shift from the problematic present to a better "future." Both projects stipulated that legitimate and proper creativity could be manifested, instituted, and presented through instituting designers with formal education and qualifications, as well as by helping seamstresses to develop artisan-quality stitching skills. These state and NGO projects reflect and contribute to the general perception of current practices in Dongdaemun that my interlocuters responded to in the stories in this chapter.

While I initially had the similar perception of Dongdaemun's fast-fashion production and global fast fashion in general as being demoralizing for workers because of the replicated designs and repetitious stitching work, during my fieldwork, I encountered numerous workers who talk about their love for making clothes. While finding extensive evidence of the burdens of fast-paced work, which challenged and brought hardship to the working lives of designers and stitching workers, I also had to attend to and make sense of accounts that give the other side of story, explaining why they still sustain their labor despite the burden and the widespread critique of repetitive and replicative works. For instance, as Eunae asserted earlier in this chapter, one cannot sustain the intensity of working in Dongdaemun without having any passion for it. While the work was often denigrated by outsiders as being purely imitative, many people said they felt affection, attachment, or excitement when dealing with clothes. They were passionate about their work.

Taking my cue from the very terms my interlocutors use, I call the practices of the workers in Dongdaemun "passionate imitation." Passionate imitation brings together contradictory ethnographic and analytic concepts that shape the meanings around the fast-paced work my interlocutors perform. In using the word "passion," I do not intend to romanticize the workers' practices but to reveal these contradictions and highlight an aspect of their work that has been overshadowed by external critiques and dominant perceptions of labor conditions. "Passion" is an ethnographic term that designers and seamstresses used during our conversations, through which they tried to explain their own attachment to work and their desire to create "a normative" space to belong that otherwise seemed impossible to exist. Simultaneously, in the ethnographic sense, the concept of "imitation" illuminates the ways in which designers and seamstresses accept critiques of their work as copies yet still perform their work with passion, care, and attachment. Garment workers have a temporally and spatially proximate relationship to the clothes they make, creating new forms, shapes, and relationships with their work, which may be subtle but are often innovative. Above all, my interlocutors discuss their work as implicitly creative, but without attempting to affix an external frame of creation, as I explore in this chapter.

Through these stories, I suggest that we must rethink imitation and consider it in a broader sense that goes beyond the dualistic frame of copying and designing. By attending to imitation in its multiple forms, rather than including them in the category of creation, the chapter challenges the hegemonic and privileged status of "creativity." As the sociologist Gabriel Tarde discusses in his theory of society and modern economic exchange, imitation can be viewed as a continuous invisible transmission of feelings and exchange of persuasions and excitement through media, knowledge, or materials (Latour and Lépinay 2009). For Tarde, economic and social exchange consists of individual actors' constant repetition that constantly creates subtle differences from one another. With these subtle differences, imitation is never perfect and thus contains within it a potential surplus that allows an event or an action to deviate into invention (Barry and Thrift 2007, 517). This imitation can also be seen in reference to the broader social exchange that my interlocutors take part in by producing and circulating nonbrand clothes. While the brand logic of creativity divides the creative from the imitative in dichotomous ways, my interlocutors touch on the ambiguity between the two. They also conduct broadly defined copying and sampling practices of other peoples' work, many of them eventually producing innovative designs, and see their work as generating materially and symbolically "meaningful" differences. The particular conditions of fast production in the marketplace, as I explore, allows us to see those differences. Those who make clothes articulate their own passion for developing "good skills" and making "good products," unintentionally amplifying the range of meanings that "imitation" may carry.

Imitation in Continuum

Imitation abounds in Dongdaemun. People use different words to talk about imitation, like *kapi* (copy), *imiteisyeon* (imitation), *jjaga* (fake), or *mojo* (counterfeit or replication). But not all imitations are the same. Some clothes are original, taking nothing from existing brand clothes, while others are pure copies. However, in Dongdaemun, it is hard to tell where the line is between innovation and imitation. Walking through the marketplace, day or night, one can choose from numerous (sometimes excessively so) cheap, copied versions of the latest fashion trends the instant they hit the stores. In some cases, the designers and seamstresses in Dongdaemun are able to create new styles in only two days. It is possible to see a new style of jacket on a popular TV show on Friday night, find a very similar item in Dongdaemun by Saturday night, and peruse endless variations on that style the following week. Other imitations are not exact copies of particular garments but show loose connections to the styles of famous designers (figure 3.1). Some even speak to the images of famous people. For example, some shops display walls of jeans each with a sign bearing the name of a K-pop star who inspired the garment (figure 3.2). You might find a women's knitwear store, like the one in

FIGURE 3.1. Ambiguous imitation 1: shirts hanging on the wall of a retail store. The tags at each neckline are transliterations of mostly foreign luxury brand names written in Korean letters. Some index the logo of a particular design, but others do not.

Photo by Ha Young Park.

FIGURE 3.2. Ambiguous imitation 2: pants hanging on the wall of a retail store. Each tag displays the names of Korean singers and actors, conveying that the pants are their "style."

Photo by the author.

figure 3.1, with product signs on each garment that transliterate famous designer brands into Korean characters. Some stores display purses and handbags without any signs indicating the brands but with familiar logos on the top and patterns on the leather, like the Gucci or Louis Vuitton insignias. However, there are countless other stores with labels that cannot be found anywhere else; they are original to Dongdaemun.

Brand names, when they are legitimately credited or illegitimately copied, operate as material markers, a recognized style, or simply the particular meanings that they carry like "cool" or "stylish." The anthropologist Constantine Nakassis (2012b) describes a complex spectrum of brand value in which the ontologies of commodities range from the real, to deauthorized gray-market commodities, to various degrees of counterfeit and nonbrand commodities, based on his research of local ready-made clothes in the Tamil Nadu region of South India. Instead of the dichotomous understanding of "counterfeit" and "original brand" goods, Nakassis (2012a, 705) suggests that we see commodities as "aesthetics of brandedness," having *loose affiliations* to authorized brand instances "through fractional similitude to them" and thus "looking *like* brand commodities." The clothes that I observed in Dongdaemun range from explicit counterfeit goods to mostly nonbrand clothes. In South Korea, nonbrand clothes are associated with Dong-daemun and often vaguely linked with imitation clothes. The history of Korea's garment industry shapes the range of nonbrand clothes and makes its aesthetics of brandedness more complicated.

In Dongdaemun, a brand name does not necessarily equate with originality of the clothes nor signify those who initiated and governed the manufacturing process of the clothes. When Dongdaemun was the star of the state-led develop-mental economic plans in the 1960s and 1970s, the South Korean state pushed forward its role as a prominent OEM (original equipment manufacturer) as a way to promote export-centered production. Factories imported textiles and materi-als from global apparel brands, such as Nike or Adidas, fabricated the clothes, and exported the final product back to the brand without the original manufacturer's name. The international division of labor affected the formation of the local mar-ket in many manufacturing countries by generating an "export-surplus" that circulates and is bought in the local markets, as well as by providing the "design templates or models" from which local producers design their clothes (Nakassis 2012a, 709–10). In South Korea, outsourcing and OEM factories became the founda-tion of a wholesale market for domestic consumers. Although the clothes produced there were supposed to be confined within the tax-free zone of the OEM, clothes regularly "spilled out" of the OEM factory zones. Gradually, clothes made be-yond the strict boundaries of the OEM zone were called *bose* clothes. The phrase, *boryu gwanse* in Korean, often abbreviated to *bose*, refers to "suspended tax." While *bose* was originally used to refer to any clothes made in Korea for foreign companies, it has gradually come to refer to clothes without a recognizable brand name in general.

In the 1980s, as the Korean domestic apparel market expanded, entrepreneur-ial designers and wholesale owners in Dongdaemun began to actively produce their own designs. In addition to properly trademarked, high-priced designer brands (typically referred to as top-tier clothes) and more medium-priced, ca-sual brands (second tier), bose clothes formed the third tier of the South Korean domestic apparel market. Gradually, as formal ready-made Korean brands (first and second tier) increasingly filled department stores, malls, and boutiques, people started to mix *bose* with *sijang ot* (marketplace clothes) or *Dongdaemun ot* (Dong-daemun clothes). In short, "Dongdaemun clothes" has become a synonym for all these categories of nonbrands and local, independent brands in general. I borrow the term "nonbrand" from Nakassis, who defined it as "forms that don't refer-ence any existing brand but have the formal structure of a branded garment." People sometimes say "bose brand" or "Dongdaemun brand," which might sound contradictory to the category of nonbrand clothes. The brand names of these clothes would rarely be recognized, except for a few cases. Once they become well enough known to be recognized, they would no longer be considered bose, sijang, or Dongdaemun clothes.[4]

Throughout this historical process, a brand name and logo gradually came to mean a coherent system of trademark. Jinsoo, a shop owner who has run a garment label business for ready-made and custom-made brands in Dongdaemun for the last sixteen years, has witnessed these changes. In the 1970s and 1980s, in addition to producing garment labels by order, he used to invent brand names, selling his ready-made labels to Dongdaemun wholesalers. Discussing his experience, Jinsoo looked back on his business:

[handwritten: outsource work like the call-time workers; here they talk something for themselves]

> At the beginning of my business, I made the label for a foreign company that outsourced its manufacturing to Dongdaemun factories. The factory owners affixed random labels for the clothes that were manufactured from copies of a sample design. I twisted famous names—you know, like "LEBIS" from "Levi's." My staff and I sometimes came up with random ones. At one point, there were many clothes being sold in Dongdaemun with my own name! Isn't that funny? The wholesalers and factory owners didn't know much about the names and just repeated the label as they filled orders for overseas companies. *[handwritten: is this illegal?]*

Over time, Jinsoo was able to observe how the different units that manufacture and distribute clothes work together. After fulfilling orders placed by Korean or overseas companies, the wholesale manufacturers bought ready-made labels, like those that Jinsoo designed, and stitched them onto their copies of those products. The labels themselves became an accessory that was thought to confirm the clothes had been produced appropriately. Even when the factory owners made their own designs, making brand names and claiming the right to ownership of the design was not a big concern. Recently, with the increasing presence of online stores, customers tend to come to Jinsoo to create a unique brand name and label design.

However, in many ways, designing in Dongdaemun still remains invisible. One day when I dropped by the store to chat, Jinsoo showed me an "order form" for a denim jacket from a famous Korean apparel brand. He said the wholesaler who was producing the jacket had designed the jacket and created a sample that already sported the logo of the Korean apparel company. The Korean company decided to order a small batch of five thousand pieces. After completing the purchase, the company then created a retroactive order form with the jacket design to set up the false sequence that the company itself had invented the design prior to outsourcing its production. That is, not only was the logo attached later, but the company also *drew the design sketch after the fact.* The design order form could potentially be used if the company decided to order more of the designed item as a way to formalize and expedite the sampling and outsourcing process. Together, the Korean apparel company, the Dongdaemun wholesaler, and Jinsoo, the label creator, worked together to design and brand the jacket—and then to create the proper paper trail.[5] This example illustrates informal practices that I frequently observed in Dongdaemun and are also commonly found at many other garment-outsourcing sites.

The nonbrandness of Dongdaemun's clothes come in a wide spectrum, from explicit knock-offs of well-known brand logos and designs, to ambiguous usages of brand logos, the use of unknown names, or even simply original designs that do not reference any brand. The distinctions become obscured because of the lack of formally recognized brand names unique to the marketplace and the immediate dispersion of one style. Even the significant presence of innovative designs is not generally recognized in Dongdaemun. Due to its export-centered production history and its reputation as a place to find just-in-time clothes, to many observers, and even to the workers and traders involved in the production of the design, *creativity* has always been seen as lacking in the image and trajectories of Dongdaemun. However, as discussed in this section, counterfeit or imitation goods are "semiotically rich" (Pang 2008), and so is the work of making the imitative goods, broadly defined. Extending recent scholarship that documents and analyzes the complex semiotics and ontology of counterfeit goods that challenge a dichotomous notion of the original and the imitation,[6] I focus on the varying meanings of "imitation" as verb in the following sections. I ask what is the nature of the practice of making an imitation for the garment designers and seamstresses I encounter. By looking at the processes of garment making that my informants frame as "imitation" yet still perform with passion, it is possible to see the problems with the hierarchical dichotomy of creation and imitation that is associated with garment design and manufacture, branded and nonbranded clothes, and Korea's place in the global economy.

Encounters through Design Work

During my fieldwork I followed three designers throughout their workdays and interviewed more than twenty other workers who identified themselves as "designers." For clothes sold in Dongdaemun, in many cases, wholesale stores take a central role in initiating designs and outsourcing manufacturing. Designers open their own stores or work for stores, where their "design work" is far from desk work. An experienced designer, like Jiyoung (who had worked for seven years in Dongdaemun), takes on a role that is more typical of merchandisers in an apparel company, including coming up with a production plan, designing the clothes, and procuring all the materials. Designers would also often take on the role of a factory manager, arranging and overseeing the assembly processes of different divisions of garment manufacturing. Many young women with various degrees of design experience are hired by wholesale owners or start their own business. By following the designers' activities, I came into contact with almost everybody involved in the process of creating a single garment, a process that is highly fragmented and specialized. Each of the production phases and the various actors who produce a garment are spread out around Dongdaemun. Running alongside the designers, I traced the complicated network that links the fabric and material wholesalers, the stitching factories, the finishing factories, the washing factories, and the embroiderers, all of whom ultimately contribute to producing a finished product.

In Dongdaemun, designers coordinate the manufacturing process from inception to the end product. The constant mobility of their work does not allow time "gaps" in the twenty-four-hour running of the market. For each item, a trained designer either develops her own idea or goes to a retail store to buy an item to use as a "sample." One day I followed Jiyoung and Hyeju (another younger designer working for their store, Angel) as they created an article of clothing. Acting like a regular shopper (and warning me in advance that I should also act casual), Jiyoung bought a sample item from Doota, a retail mall. Then she went directly to get materials and garment parts, like buttons and zippers, to copy from the sample. If the store did not have enough of what she needed, she quickly moved on to the next store or improvised a new plan to fit the available stock, since she could not wait for the materials to be ordered. Designers run from wholesaler to wholesaler picking out what they need and have the items promptly delivered to a stitching factory or take the packages there themselves. Having the packages delivered meant that the designers simply put a sticker with their store name, Angel, and the stitching factory name, Danseong-sa, with a telephone number. Jiyoung called her quick-service delivery agency, whose deliverymen are always standing by and instantly came to pick up the package. The item then moved from one factory to another to be assembled. After it was completed, the designer continued to work with the factory workers and owners on revisions, and the final product was then delivered to the wholesale nighttime market. In her normal daily routine, a designer deals with one or two items already in production, as well as a new item being designed and developed as a sample.

In addition to overseeing product development, designers were providing a great deal of emotional care for their colleagues. They were constantly buying snacks, smiling, listening to complaints about work and personal life, and so on. A designer's phone is constantly ringing for updates on the work process and deliveries. A mobile phone connects their work and virtually expands production time. Jiyoung said she receives nearly one hundred calls a day from their employer (wholesale store owners), motorbike delivery people, factory owners, or textile and garment accessory wholesale store owners to check the orders and deliveries. Many designers said that it is an implicit but very strict rule to respond to calls even after they go back home and go to bed, while the nighttime wholesale market is running.[7] Extra batteries or chargers are a must-carry item. As there is no standardized center for the manufacturing processes, all information and transactions are managed by designers with their phones and in their movements throughout the market. It was after a few months after Hyeju was hired that Jiyoung transferred the list of all the important contact numbers of these diverse actors in the marketplace to Hyeju's mobile phone, representing a sign of trust.

Our conversations and Jiyoung's work were often interrupted by various phone calls, and one-third of the calls were to appease small complaints and bickering between actors in the marketplace or just listen to people's chatting. If one individual slows down, another cannot start on time, and the whole process falls behind amid the pressing pace of daily production. I noticed that Jiyoung had adopted a familial friendliness and informality in her tone of voice and attitude by using kinship terms, such as "imo" [auntie], "samchon" [uncle], and "eonni" [sister] with her colleagues. She remembered the intricate family systems that connect these actors and was sensitive toward the age hierarchy, in-law relationships, and personal issues from their family history. Jiyoung shared these important "work tips" with her junior partner, Hyeju. This rapport and inside knowledge enabled Jiyoung to quickly assess the availability of materials from sellers whose stock changes daily and to check on how the work was being completed in each factory, all the while avoiding tensions and glitches. The complicated supply chain requires attention and flexibility to proceed smoothly. Jiyoung said she raises her voice and speaks quickly to keep herself and her counterparts constantly moving forward and maintain a sense of tension and energy.

Walking the Design, Meaningful Difference

Shepherding the garments from concept to sale, the designers have intense interactions with their clothes. This enables them to recognize their own products, as they are being sold and dispersed throughout the market. Unlike "sampling," which means designers start with a sample product bought from a different store or brand-name clothes, an order form with an elaborate "design sketch" would be material evidence of "originality," a piece that was started from scratch. Jiyoung proudly showed me her order forms, which often contained sketches. Jiyoung was designing a long vest from scratch and had multiple drawings and revised order forms. Even for the jacket that she copied from a sample, she made a simple sketch reflecting changes she made. As copied designs spread out in the marketplace, designers' attachment to the clothes and the improvisation they make in the design evolve together throughout their daily activities in Dongdaemun. In describing her involvement in the design, Jiyoung said: "You saw how much I carried that one item here and there. I chose the thread, buttons, and everything and sent them to the factory. I examined the original in even more detail than the original designer who drew the sketch. I designed it while working with people—the market people who are really dealing with the clothes, not those who are working in the office. . . . So it *only gets better.*"

The frenetic lines crisscrossing the market in the walking map (figure 3.3) are not merely lines of movement from one location to another; rather, they map the trajectories of interaction with other actors in the market and the body that moves along with the commodity as having designed and adding layers of "betterment." Each time she interacts with other actors Jiyoung infuses new ideas into the clothes. Unlike when she used to work for a big apparel company, where her designs would find their way to the shelf two seasons later, Jiyoung was thrilled to see her clothes on shelves and displays across Dongdaemun's retail stores within two nights. This quick pace of materializing her idea and circulating the material product to the space creates more frequent and immediate tempos that designers work with their product. The short cycles of return and the short cycles of interaction with others create more frequent contacts and fill the marketplace with dense connections between people and commodities, in contrast to the generalized understanding of fast-paced flexible production as distancing and alienating human labor.

[margin note:] feel closer to their work w/ more immediate satisfaction

Designers, when narrating their intensive and extended working experiences, often described the "thrill" (*jjaritam*) of being present, occupying and moving in the space along with material commodities, and referred to their "attachment" (*aechak*) and "passion" (*yeoljeong*). Taemin, a designer who had a long career in a top-tier apparel company in Korea, described her work there as uninspiring. After ten years Taemin became a manager of the main design team of women's boutique brands, in charge of overseeing younger designers. Taemin described the work as "exchanging good jokes, flattering executives, and drinking a lot." As a result, she began to feel distanced from the actual clothes that she devoted her entire career life to. Working in Dongdaemun, Taemin was able to have a more intimate relationship with her products. Taemin now works as a main designer for her older sister's wholesale store in Dongdaemun and takes pride in producing clothes that are "less imitative" (*deol bekkineun*). Taemin refused to call her work "original" because, she said, "nothing is new under the sky": "One way or another [whether in Dongdaemun or in a formal company], we all imitate each other. If something I make starts a trend, then that means I was already being either inspired or imitating the vibe. I'm

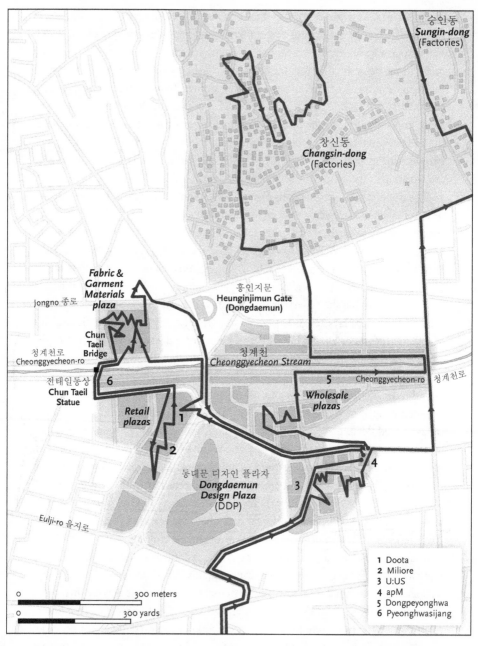

FIGURE 3.3. Jiyoung's daily movements based on my shadowing of her work and interviews. The zigzagging in and out of buildings and factories is roughly expressed.

Courtesy of Lohnes+Wright.

not even sure I can say I created an entirely original piece when I have been checking thousands of images and samples on trend. I can see how even those famous designers imitate each other. How many unique striped T-shirts can there possibly be? You just keep to the a basic level of ethics."

The unspoken but widely shared "ethics" of informal markets are not exceptional in Dongdaemun. Kedron Thomas offers a rich account of "discourse of envy" among garment merchants, as well as their neighborly kindness and mutual obligation of Guatemala (Thomas 2012). My interlocutors often called this "good consciousness" (*yangsim*) or "business morality" (*sangdodeok*) among the wholesalers and designers. The most common business morality they emphasized to wait a day to sample someone else's design. In addition, when sampling an item, it is ethical not to lower the price "too much" from the one that you copied from, even if you have a better manufacturing network to produce it at a lower cost. It is also part of the courtesy to refrain from copying from items in the same "hallway." In the wholesale malls, in which one floor houses more than a hundred cube-shaped stores, one's new designs are immediately exposed to others. Bickering occurs frequently between those who have identical items in the same hallway or on the same floor. Quite a few designers I spoke with described disputes over design ownership or "basic ethics."

But Jiyoung said, "You cannot impose the rule [the ethic], and you cannot always fight [for it]." Many designers conduct mixed practices of various registers of imitation, as Jiyoung was working on a copied jacket from sample and a long vest that she designed on her own at the same time. However, as she oversaw the various changes and made improvisations, interacting with other material traders, fabric cutters, sample makers, and seamstresses, the dichotomy between the originally designed item and the copied item from a sample product gradually becomes destabilized. Jiyoung could discern or pick out a garment that came from her design from among many others that look almost the same. Rather than feeling indignation or a sense of propriety, Jiyoung said she felt thrilled and proud when she sees the expansion of a design that she made real in the world. Echoing what Taemin mentioned above and many other similar comments from designers that I interviewed, what matters here is less about making an "invention" that has never existed before than creating and observing the recognizable differences that are disseminated and desired in the world. Amid sped-up production and circulation, designers feel animated in their up-close interactions with the material goods, as they move together with the clothes in every single step of subtle changes and see the clothes filling up the hangers and shelves of the marketplace. And this proximity and immediacy furthers the attachment that workers have with their creations, enough to recognize the subtle differences they care about. What materializes in the rapid production schedule is not merely the scale of quantity and illegitimate hijacking of other's original ideas. It is, rather, designers keeping the intricate manufacturing network affectively tied to their embodied mobility and engagement with their clothes. This design work shifts the focus of creativity from a regime of trademark to the rich interactions between people, ideas, and materials, generating divergences and improvisations.

Naming Clothes and Ambiguous Imitation

Due to the numerous different forms of nonbrand clothes and their mixture with explicit knock-offs, my interlocutors always had to explain how their production was different from appropriating the signature patterns of designer brands or illegally using their logos. However, this did not mean that they use only original names in the production process. Famous designer names, such as Donna Karan, Chanel, or Calvin Klein, are often used to identify or classify designs that may not have anything to do with those brands. On one of the days I was following Jiyoung's daily routine, I learned that she and Hyeju dub their products something like "Donna Karan long vest" or "Chanel leather jacket" instead of using a numeric or alphabetical product code. They did it just for convenience; it did not matter that the vest had nothing to with Donna Karan. I have never seen any Donna Karan reference in the course of Jiyoung's designing and selling the vest— and the name Donna Karan is not used when the jacket is sold in the retail malls. This name could be used on a jacket sign when it goes to the show windows in retail stores but may also be used only as a reference among the designers and wholesalers without ever reaching the customer.

This example was at one extreme end of the range of attitudes that Dongdaemun producers have about being categorized as "imitation makers." The other extreme end of this would be designers like Taemin, who earlier contrasted her experiences working in a major apparel company and in Dongdaemun; such designers sought to brand their own clothes by using their own names and unique codes consistently throughout the whole process—from their store names, to the tags attached to the clothes, to the names they use to identify each item, to the name they use when displaying the piece on the walls of the store. Despite these formal practices, their brand names would hardly be recognized once their clothes were sold via different retailers and buried with thousands of other nonbrand clothes. Figure 3.1, at the beginning of this chapter, shows a retail store where famous brand names are not directly attached to the clothes but instead used on the display wall to draw customer attention. The associated clothing item may have nothing to do with the designer name but is used for easy communication with the customers, who might ask, "Could you show me that Chanel T-shirt?"

to identify the particular item out of fifteen different T-shirts on display. The name brand may also give a hint of trendiness, although it is extremely ambiguous whether there are any qualities and traits of a Chanel design aesthetic imbued in the shirt.

The dichotomy of "imitation" and "creation" plays out in multiple ways within the hierarchical structure of design and name branding. In the case of Angel, designers framed their performance as a sort of imitation by giving it someone else's name. This kind of imitation does not intend to replicate the name brand or reference any particular component of the aesthetics. What is imitated here is not the content of the design but rather the landscape of the fashion industry, where brand names precede design content. The use of brand names, including their abuses, misuses, and ambiguous uses, are copious in various landscapes of the fashion industry. By casually denominating and packaging their clothes as knock-offs, they turn their work into a second-class type of clothing. This indifferent use of brand names defies the broader intellectual property regime and also the social value associated with creativity as a dominant frame to account for customer satisfaction and appeal of the brand designs or subjective fulfillment and motivations of the work. In this local fast-fashion market at the margins of the domestic and global garment industry, where the "original" producer is hard to trace or is invisible, "names" surface out of the deep layer of innumerable variations and differentiations of designs, intricate networks of outsourcing, and the vivid attachment and buried creative desires of producers.

Stitching the Design

I first met Heejung in a sewing class organized by MANI. Like many other seamstresses I met during my fieldwork, Heejung started working in Dongdaemun when she was a teenager and has worked there for more than thirty years. While she was working in stitching factories as a head seamstress or sample maker (which requires the highest level of sewing skills in the factory), Heejung was taking MANI's advanced garment skill class at night and was planning to take more design and alteration classes. Her plan was to gradually train herself to design clothes and open her own retail store someday. Mr. Nam, the instructor and mentor of the class, though, was very skeptical of this idea. He asked, "Why don't you just focus on the sewing [instead of trying to design on her own]? You have very good stitching skills. Designing your own thing is not so easy to accomplish, and you cannot just become a designer that way."

Mr. Nam's skepticism was not merely his own opinion. The MANI classes were designed to promote the dignity of laborers so that they can gain satisfaction

Similar to the [...] [...] ready → not intended for them to dream of more, but they see the upward mobility

via the subjective processes of labor. Seamstresses learn the whole process from garment design, to pattern making, to stitching and assembly (a process that is fragmented in the traditional production process). The purpose of the curriculum was to connect the seamstresses to their own labor and other laborers. In the ideal vision of MANI, seamstresses work from 9:00 a.m. to 5:00 p.m.; get individually recognized, respected, and remunerated as craftspeople for their stitching skills; and have equal discussions about the work with other garment experts, such as pattern makers and designers. From the activists' perspective, this would give the workers the time and support to produce "creative" goods and perform meaningful work, instead of merely repeating dull tasks.[8] For this reason, the staff, board members, garment experts, and labor activists were concerned that participants more interested in being entrepreneurs would become distracted from the organizational goal of developing a pool of artisan-level garment seamstresses and would perpetuate Dongdaemun's existing problems of discredited imitation and poor-quality products.

It is within this frame of wage labor that MANI conceptualized "proper work," while opposing the current marginalization and devaluation of garment stitching workers. Even though they are invested in empowering garment workers and raising social recognition of the care, hard work, and rigorous training that were needed for the current experienced seamstresses to become professionals, MANI continued to frame its project goal within the stable category of jobs. In their idealized understanding of the production process, designers would produce a professional concept, and this design would be meticulously realized through the high-caliber stitching skills or craftsmanship that MANI encouraged the seamstresses to achieve in their training. MANI's organization and its efforts to intervene in the market are discussed in depth in chapter 4.

Yet many participants' dreams and current practices deviate from the norms that MANI pursued. The media often covers dramatic success stories of small factories or wholesale stores that rose to prominence in the apparel industry, including South Korean denim brands like Jambangee, BASIC, and BangBang. Most of my interlocutors did not aim that high but often talked about hoping to sell just one or two items that they had designed. This dream was a possibility since many people in the market had experienced this type of mobility. Manufacturing factories, wholesale stores, and retail malls are not that rigidly divided but connected through family and other close networks, and people often move from one role to another. I often met seamstresses in Changsin-dong who had worked as a designer for a wholesale business.

I saw Heejung again one year later at a reunion. She was very excited to share her recent design experience with the group. Heejung's employer, having recently contracted with Russian businessmen for a large order of innovative designs, asked her to come up with a variety of design samples. Although she was a seamstress, no other designers were readily available, and Heejung jumped at the chance. To her surprise, Heejung's designs were a hit. The contented Russians ordered more, and the factory owner asked Heejung to come up with new samples. Like many other seamstresses, Heejung frequently moved from one factory to another and had dealt with various customers from Korea and overseas. Russians traders have been frequent customers. She recalled her experience: "It seemed like the Russians liked very flamboyant and flowery patterns, maybe like those from ten to twelve years ago. I vaguely knew that because I used that pattern a lot when I first started working. . . . Since I don't know about Korean designs for youth, I think it's easier for me to be creative in their [Russian] sense. But who knows if they will like my next samples or not. I just patched together my random ideas as I remember them." It seemed like this moment gave her more confidence to dream about opening her own store and optimism about her current work, even without formal education or training in design. Heejung's long-held dream of producing her own design seemed to come one step closer to reality in this sudden opportunity to design for Russian consumers. While this experience is particular to Heejung, it is common to the narratives of seamstresses and, consequently, the nature of design in Dongdaemun.

Fashion is a fickle business, and it is not always clear which patterns, ruffles, buttons, or stitches will win over consumers. Moreover, Dongdaemun's manufacturing structure and complicated network of outsourced factories are constantly in flux and in need of just-in-time adaptations to meet customer's immediate desires. In this context, anticipation and calculation are not the most important aspects of bringing a product to market. The fast pace of the market and the changeability of design rely on experienced workers who have a keen awareness of and attachment to their products and skills.

Seamstresses often worked independently, with only one or two assistants, subcontracted to the manufacturing networks and mastering numerous kinds of clothing, from fabric pieces to whole clothes. While a seamstress's job is to repeat the same task hundreds of thousands of times, proper repetition should be invisible. Yet a seamstress comes to feel that they know, discern, and create a good design and even desire to make one.

Increasing Number, Expanding Passion

In the stitching and manufacturing of clothes, seamstresses create commodities fast and rigorously and motivate themselves. Just like the designers in Dongdaemun, seamstresses can also have thorough and intimate experiences with their clothes, while these caring acts serve a critical role in production and circulation in Dongdaemun. Like the designers, the seamstresses' narrations and interpretations of their work respond to the assumption that garment labor is a machine-like, mind-numbing, and repetitive job. In the previous chapter, I described how the labor process in the 1970s and 1980s led sewing workers to develop a sense of mastery and entrepreneurship to continue to work in the Dongdaemun manufacturing scene, despite their difficult labor conditions. While there is less of a master-apprentice relationship in the top-tier designer brand model, the structure enables workers to respond quickly to flexible fashion trends with a variety of new designs. But even so, many of the Korean seamstresses currently working in factories and home-factories near Dongdaemun refer to themselves as the "last generation." This is because they have witnessed the number of sewing workers decreasing and have had few younger trainees follow them. This sense of the growing marginalization of their skills can provoke a defensive response among seamstresses. Most seamstresses in the market started working in the late 1960s to the 1980s, making their way through apprenticeships to a master level in the hopes of obtaining a *gisuljik* (skilled job). Many of those whom I interviewed were trying to make sense of their own life-long investment in this occupation.

Oksun, the seamstress I discussed in the introduction, told me one day, "You should not equate garment skills with work in construction or mechanical work; garment skills need more softness and sensitive treatment," as she, like many of my informants, tried to make distinctions between their work and other forms of manufacturing labor. In the context of sewing work—the long hours, low income, and image of it as obsolete—it was hard for the workers to develop a sense of pride and formal recognition of "skill." Those who have worked for a significant amount of time in the industry narrated their complex love for the garments they make and the skills they have developed.

The "close" link between the garments and the workers manifests in the daily rhythms of the working space that create a sense of craftsmanship and mastery. Sung-Ah had worked in a home-factory in Jang'an-dong (a neighborhood near Dongdaemun market) since she started at sixteen years old. After twenty years of working, her husband started his own business, and the family moved out of Seoul. Sang-Ah kept her little home-factory but no longer has any assistants or other seamstresses. Everyday around 9 p.m., a small factory nearby that operates as a subcontractor (mediating between the wholesalers and individual seamstresses) brings the fabric pieces, which Sang-Ah sometimes cuts herself. The next morning, she starts sewing pieces and then works all day. As the finished clothes start to pile up (as many as seventy or eighty pieces in one day), Sang-Ah feels more and more satisfaction. That accomplishment of "putting together and creating anew" (*moaseo hanaro mandeuneun geo*) parallels the "quantity" she sews.

My husband says that it still amazes him that tons of little pieces come together at the end of the day. I feel the same way too. I start my day with piles of pieces that are nothing by themselves. But through my work with this one old machine, they are put together to become what covers people's bodies. Young people from foreign countries! . . . And I am still healthy and efficient, and I keep up with the rhythm. . . . I put on the radio, work quietly in this small space on my own, and end my day with finished products, something that can be immediately used. I don't need to be directed and supervised, and I don't have to deal with others.

The feeling of accomplishment she gets when she sees the final product has structured her daily life for a long time, and her confidence in dealing with various kinds of designs and items led her to develop a narrative of her work as a type of craftsmanship. When a colorful nylon fitted jacket was a big winter hit in Korea in 2008 to 2009, Sung-Ah worked nonstop without breaks and made 6,000,000 won (approximately $5,000) a month—almost three times what she usually made. During this rare and memorable time, when she commuted to her factory, she constantly ran into young people who were shopping in Dongdaemun while wearing almost the exact same jacket that she was making. Sung-Ah described these moments of immediate and physical encounters with her own products to explain to me why she would not quit her job and how she now places greater value on what she does. Sung-Ah interprets the speed of production and circulation through her own observations and encounters with the commodities that spread out and fill the spaces of the market. In this subjective sense, the space is dense with materials that she feels connected to.

Garment work and the passion workers feel for it give rise to moments in which they redefine their relationship to the commodity in the space of the market at large. Once they learned that I had studied in the United States, Sang-Ah and many other seamstresses asked me about "master" craftsmen and wanted to know how skilled workers were treated in other countries. "Korea is doing much better than before, so there will be more chance that Korea can become that same way [in which current garment workers would have a social status as craftsman], right?" Sung-Ah had dreamed about moving to Australia, where her husband's friend is in the garment industry. She was excited to hear that there were not many people working in the manufacturing industry in Australia and that seamstresses were highly valued. While the "old skill" of sewing was obsolete in Korea, Sung-Ah wanted to confirm that in other countries, especially in the more "advanced places," the "skill" of sewing would be more respected as a craft.

they crave more respect

Just Imitation

Later in that conversation, Minjae, the youngest seamstress at the table, asked Heejung, "So are you a designer now?" Everybody burst into laughter at Minjae's naivete. Minjae also laughed, but pushed, "Well, why not?" Heejung wrapped up the conversation by assuring everyone that she was not offended by their laughter. "I just did some imitation [*hyungnaeman naengeoji*]," she said, but also added, "but now and then I add something. I make it different. That's what keeps me going."

Sitting at the sewing machine, Heejung does more than piece rags together: her excitement and engagement in the process of designing anew carves out pathways that enable the market and commerce in Dongdaemun to flow. It was unclear whom exactly Heejung was referring to having imitated; likely she meant she had just "acted like a designer." Without any design sketches, she would not be recognized as a formal designer. However, she did not directly "copy" anybody else. Nobody at that table asked how she was able to do that kind of design improvisation successfully, as they might have had a similar experience in the past. As the marketplace has evolved over the past few decades, seamstresses who started their career as teenagers have taken on many different roles as traders, designers, and retailers in the intricate, intimate network of the market.

Heejung's experience creating a successful blouse not only reveals her flexible capability to produce garments across the artificial division between creative and manual labor. This openness to the transformation and the meaningful differences they produce is implicated in the practices of my interlocutors, which are often framed as "imitation." The moment of invention could be a conscious act, yet it could equally result from the unanticipated conjunction of imitative currents. At the same time, Heejung did not seem to be interested in claiming credit for this nor for further pursuing a clearly defined path as a designer or a seamstress. Her statement highlights both the possibilities and limits of her work since the experience was meaningful in making some difference in her working life. However, she seemed also to be aware that such shifts do not guarantee any change in one's position within the market; nor do they provoke any belief in a radical transformation of oneself. Instead, the subtle change that she felt sustains her in work and counteracts the limited notion of replication and repetition.

The designs Heejung and Jiyoung made and the way they framed their own work as "imitation" explain why garment manufacturing still has an active presence in Seoul, a capital city filled with cutting-edge mobile devices and high-speed networks, LED screens in the streets, global investment banks, and 24-hour shopping malls and entertainment plazas. On the one hand, the skills designers and seamstresses have cultivated in the market exceed mere sketching or stitching. On the other hand, their narratives remind us of the unyielding structural conditions under which their work takes place, including the occupational hierarchies, regions, and locations in the global fashion and garment industry, as well as the powerful regime of authorized creativity.

Conclusion

Starting with a contextualization for passionate imitation as an uneasy coupling of words when describing sped-up garment production and circulation, this chapter has also juxtaposed two parallel ethnographic accounts of designers and seamstresses. The two groups' narratives first detailed their work, through which they showed passion for "making clothes," and their seeming denouncement of their own work as imitation. Through this juxtaposition, I intended to critically engage with the discursive and structural hierarchy that surrounds their work: the hierarchy between designing and manufacturing as well as the hierarchy between creativity and imitation.

Passion is unlikely in garment manufacturing, not only because of the long-standing marginalization of garment labor but also because the labor is understood to be temporally and spatially obsolete in the contemporary economic landscape of South Korea. While seamstresses were considered to be engaged in mindless and repetitive work, the longtime investment in their skills and work led them to handle various clothes in a broad range of styles and trends, sometimes enough to add their ideas and improvisations. Similarly devalued, the designers' work making unrecognized nonbrand clothes showed rich layers of their devotion to and satisfaction in generating their ideas onto the material work, based on thick layers of in-person interactions with the various actors in the supply chain. Although the social hierarchy is strongly evident between the works of these two groups, the narratives of their own attachment to clothes and their multiple engagements with various registers of garment making unsettle the stereotypical division between their work as being purely manual or mental. The fast production and circulation of Dongdaemun heavily relies on designers' and seamstresses' performance of their work as they form a strong material and affective attachment to their own skills and products. Rather than pure estrangement, the material speed is conditioned by and furthers the immediacy and proximity between people, space, and material goods. The quick mobility of designers, the short time span of interaction with their material goods, and the repeating fashion cycles thicken the material, physical, and affective connections people have with their own work.

In capturing these thick layers of work, the analyses did repeat the privilege of creativity not only as a description of work but as an analytic frame of work. The symbolic process that labels my informants' work as imitation is not simply a lack of creativity; it involves a perceived evolutionary structure within a global garment outsourcing system in which a formal manufacturing hub like South Korea has been located and the hierarchy of economic spaces determined by the regime of brand names and intellectual property regulation. Within this, the rapidity in designing and stitching allowed Dongdaemun to thrive but also produced a problematic perception that the work cannot be original and caring. The way the state and NGO projects envision creativity for the future is also based on the narrow definition of trademarked work; it constantly disengages and marginalizes designers' and seamstresses' current practices, which showed a great amount of care and a broad continuum between imitation and creation. And as the narratives show, people in the "field"—both of ethnography and of the fashion and garment industry—are well aware of this structural limitation.

Passionate imitation is an ethnographic lens through which we account for the emotional and affective aspects of economic processes that my interlocutors participate in and their subjective interpretation of work, and understand how their narration responds to the dominant perspectives that undervalue their creative work. Instead of trying to move toward the narrow version of creation or reiterate the authority of brand regime, my interlocutors dwell in the notion of making "imitation," amplifying the complex and multifaceted features of the term. Staying with the frame of imitation, casually and deliberately, allows them to fully engage with the time-space that is connected to their own mobility and practice, as well as the commodity, and allows us to see the meaningful differences they bring about through their affective and embodied attachment and care in the present.

Part 2

PROBLEMATIZATION OF SPEED

REDIRECTING THE FUTURE

During my preliminary fieldwork in summer 2006, I was taking one of my regular walking routes through the area of Dongdaemun market, when I found a banner for the NGO MANI. The intricate mass of electric wires, haphazardly fixed to the old electric poles and decaying buildings over the years, signified the presence of home-factories and garment manufacturing outsourcing networks in the neighborhood. Through the dense bundles of wires, I spotted the green fabric banner recruiting participants for their sewing advancement classes. It popped out in the landscape; the font design, color scheme, and message did not blend with the old-fashioned signboards and facades of the buildings. The classes were designed for local garment workers with the aim of improving both their skills and working conditions. Acting on a hunch that MANI could be an effective entry point to connect with the garment workers dispersed throughout the neighborhood, I decided to contact the NGO. It was a typical "cold approach" that many ethnographers undertake; I was seeking to participate in the classrooms and offering to volunteer assisting the staff members with administrative work.

As I learned later, the feeling in this new space of awkwardness, anxiety, and exhilaration with which I approached MANI was similar to the feeling that some of my interlocutors had about finding the banner and applying for the classes. I made a blunt self-introduction; when I revisited them in 2007 for two months and then again in 2008 for fifteen months of extensive fieldwork, I was allowed to participate in classes, meetings, and events, while offering ad hoc labor assistance. From this vantage point, I was able to observe MANI's efforts to respond to the long-standing marginalization of garment workers in South Korea and to bring them to the forefront of their new vision of labor advocacy and social enterprise to produce clothes at a slow, human pace.

It was an unexpected entry point to the marketplace: a roundabout channel that plugged the ethnographer and the interlocutors into the intricate network and long histories of Dongdaemun and garment making. As a part of the legacy of South Korean social activism and the labor union movement in Dongdaemun of the 1970s and 1980s, scholars and activists have sought to respond to the critiques of the labor and economic models in garment manufacturing in Dongdaemun market. MANI locates itself squarely within this tradition. The organization explicitly problematized the emphasis on fast-paced production and consumption in Dongdaemun and addressed the problem of speed as a historical issue by connecting the memories, current investments, and future anticipations of garment labor and activism. The chapter focuses on how different actors participated in this project with incongruent paces and tempos, complicating the "slowness" and shaping the meanings and politics of garment work.

MANI's leaders and staff members were from various backgrounds of social activism in South Korea and have been involved in labor unionization, political campaigns, and alternative childcare initiatives. While garment manufacturing did not occupy the central issues of labor activism in the 2000s, when many activists were focusing on migration labor and irregular and temporary employment, MANI claimed that labor issues in garment manufacturing persist and are highly relevant. Especially in Dongdaemun, MANI leaders noted that the current global garment market is characterized by an ever-increasing pressure to produce varied, complicated designs at a quick pace. Meanwhile, they also acknowledge the limitations of union organizing and militant protest in this current situation. According to MANI, the current subcontract manufacturing, consists of self-employed workers, obscures and complicates dynamics of labor and capital. While wholesalers make the most money in the supply chain, they are also in many ways the marginal independent contractors in the broader structure of the fashion and garment industry (in addition to being overworked).[1] In response, MANI leaders first started a care community that supported childcare for garment workers in the neighborhood and offered a space for them to share information and learn garment-making skills. Then it designed a market-based social enterprise to promote ethically produced clothes by domestic garment workers with decades of experiences. This profit model, which I call by the pseudo-name "the Company," created a network of experienced seamstresses, ethical and critical consumers, and social activists and entrepreneurs. The goal of both MANI's classes and the social enterprise model was to give more "time" to the seamstresses, allowing them to develop new skills and survive in the changing conditions of the garment industry. MANI promoted the workshop as an experiment in which experienced seamstresses were taught to produce clothes at a slower pace, with the goal of improving their status from "unskilled" to "high-skilled" laborers.

The fieldwork I explore in this chapter reveals that the organization was not external to the market but connected these existing actors who were actively involved in the market in a different network of slow and humane labor practice. *slow-living?* This made MANI a significant site to research, not only for the experimental project it created but also as a lens to see the broader market from a different angle. MANI's project opened up an ethnographic space in which I could filter and revisit my own findings and analyses, by exploring how activists and workers interpret and act on the temporal dimensions of work and the problem of speed.

Every Tuesday and Thursday, staff and participants in the sewing skill advancement class at MANI would meet for dinner before class. It was always at the same modest, local restaurant that offered one fixed meal and that could accommodate our large group, even when some members arrived late or were absent. The class was for experienced seamstresses to be trained in "high fashion"[2] clothes stitching that involved careful seams, complicated techniques, and refined materials. Classes started at 7:00 p.m., and many of the participants were coming back from their regular work at busy sewing factories in and around Dongdaemun or elsewhere in Seoul.

The dinner started at 6:15 p.m. and represented a temporal threshold for many of the class participants. The participants mostly worked hard at their regular workplace all day and hurried to arrive on time, frequently arriving late and leaving little time for dinner before class. Even though they are mostly self-employed seamstresses,[3] the class participants had to make arrangements with their assistants or other subcontractors to have this precious time to themselves. Once arrived at MANI, they had to change to a slow, careful, and patient working mode. Eating and chatting at the table, they would ease into a different pace and orientation to their day. In this transition, participants also shared their life stories of work and their own understanding of MANI's project and its vision.

It was at one of the dinners in April 2009 when Jonghee was chatting with me and raised a concern that was important to a number of other people at the same table. Jonghee, a woman with thirty-two years of sewing experience, had come to MANI sewing skill advancement classes with her friend. Jonghee expressed her anxieties about participating in the project and asked for my opinion:

> You have a lot of education, even abroad. So, tell us, how likely is it that this project will be successful? We only know that we were told that our skills are outstanding. Do you think that it really is enough to be recognized

from the outside, too? . . . I understand that the [MANI] staff means well and has good ideals, but what if the reward comes after I cannot work anymore? My body is getting old. I have worked in this market for forty years, and my body feels different every day. I devoted my youth to garment making and the labor movement. Don't you think I should expect some visible change and benefit from what we are doing now?

Other women in the group who had similar backgrounds and continued to be actively engaged in MANI projects had similar concerns as Jonghee. As I discussed in earlier chapters, many of them were already over the average age of retirement, having started working when they were teenagers and continuing into their fifties and sixties. These workers' valuable lifetime of experience was fundamental to MANI's project: it claims to appreciate the lifetime devotion to the garment work that set up the moral foundation for its project, and the future vision of their being treated as artisan-level workers, economically and socially, made their goal highly radical. In other words, rapid industrialization in South Korea is indebted to manufacturing workers like Jonghee, and MANI was claiming a new future for South Koreans through the transformation of these workers. However, participants were conscious about their aging bodies, which affected the hope they could maintain about their working life. For the seamstresses, slowing their work pace meant an immediate drop in their income because they are often paid by the piece, while the women's age and experience made it difficult for them to change their work rhythm. For the women in MANI's class, their hope and anxiety were framed by their embodied time.

Jonghee's and her colleagues' anxiety reveals the embedded temporal aspects of MANI's project: the disjuncture of paces the women were asked to perform, including compounded hurriedness, pressure and reluctance to move forward, and hopes and insecurity associated with one's own cycles and rhythms of work. Still, the active and persistent presence of these workers powers Dongdaemun in the city center and gave rise to MANI. This directed my ethnographic interest toward MANI's labor politics as "slowed work." I argue that MANI's slowed-down market experiment consists of and is sustained by heterogeneous investments and attachments, just like the fast pace that characterizes the regular market functions in Dongdaemun.

MANI's project incorporates the existing, hidden, and newly emerging social actors of Dongdaemun into a new network, while simultaneously embedding its practice in the place of Dongdaemun. By bringing an ethnographic sensibility to paces and temporal orientations, it is also possible to see how intersections of temporality in Dongdaemun are contingent and ironic, leading away from a simple frame of failure and success (Traweek 2009). As Hirokazu Miyazaki (2003,

255) suggests, the intersecting temporality both *opens and closes* possibilities for knowing and acting in the market for the workers and researchers.[4] This chapter highlights the incongruent paces and temporal orientations that shape MANI's projects: the engineered slow pace to challenge the labor alienation for garment workers; the funding cycle of the government policies for social enterprise, a retrospective nostalgia of former labor activists and their attachment to the past; the embodied and performed paces of participants who have been in the market for decades; and also the enduring hope of intermittent pauses that give workers a moment to rearticulate their own meanings of work. This moment would never be enough to eventually slow down the pace of market but opened up possibilities for redirected and reconnected futures that its participants could imagine.

Creating the Slow Market

Pursuing a slow pace has been a widespread goal for public and commercial initiatives related to diverse issues, ranging from food, health, scholarship, trade, and consumption to urban development. Within the popular, public, and scholarly imaginaries of these initiatives, slow pace recovers and newly creates a "better" life that modern capitalist society feels it has lost, including balance and sustainability for life on earth, human connectedness and equality, and ethically and politically improved material processes. However, as Sara Sharma (2011, 111) points out, culturally driven slowness is not outside the normalizing temporal order. Rather, in certain contexts, slowness is created and fetishized within a given temporal politics. Likewise, the kind of slowness that MANI claims was situated in the particular context of Dongdaemun and its place in the South Korean garment industry.

The slow pace claimed by MANI's activism revolves around its critique of labor alienation as caused by market competition, which they view as pressuring workers to ramp up their speed in Dongdaemun and in the garment industry in general. The accelerated production and circulation speed were seen as fundamental to the new manufacturing processes that characterize Dongdaemun and the flexible fashion industry in general today. Activists highlighted their view that consumers retain an impulse for quick fashion and that South Korean society ignores ongoing social inequality in favor of the valorization of South Korean industrialization and economic prosperity.

MANI designed what they viewed as a more ethical form of production and consumption that was meant to develop unskilled laborers into the more marketable and sustainable "artisans." Aligning with Marxist activists, the activists viewed the very structure of the labor problem to be that fast work is synchronizing and controlling of human activities to the extent that people are treated as a machine part or slaves for the obsessively fast production and circulation. In this understanding, as briefly discussed in chapter 3, stitching workers remained categorized as unskilled or low-skilled laborers who are merely doing repetitive work. Moreover, they would be in danger of being replaced by even cheaper labor or seeing their jobs outsourced to factories. Based on this sense of crisis, MANI set up the somewhat nationalistic aim to "protect" the workers from a cascade of imported goods from China, Indonesia, and Myanmar that would even further endanger current Korean garment workers.

MANI intended to solve this problem by upgrading these laborers so that they would now be considered high-skilled artisans. In the current market system, there is no time for workers to enhance their skills and no opportunity to learn from others, resulting in these workers remaining unskilled or low-skilled laborers. Among the graduates of the two semesters of sewing skill enhancement courses, select students are encouraged to take an intensification course where they learn from other artisan workers. The goal of the program was to have the participants fully connected to (1) their own labor experience, knowing what they are working on, working at their own pace, thinking about the material, and enjoying the process; (2) other laborers, knowing about them in detail, sharing meals, having breaks together, sharing ideas and reviewing their stitches; and (3) the product of their labor, the quality of the end product and taking pride in the label, which combines the artisans' name and the MANI brand logo.

The workshop came out in the broader context in which global fair trade and tourism, international donation and aid work, and ethical consumerism and co-op models emerged as booming issues in the 2000s in South Korea. While co-ops and organic food networks had a long history in South Korea's local food movement and alliance of agricultural communities, the concept of slow food became more popular when the Slow Food Conference launched in 2009 and Slow Food Korea opened its office in 2014 as part of the International Slow Food Movement. MANI's workshop likewise aligned with other slow movements and consumer trends in South Korea by bringing into collaboration individual consumers and organizations in these fields. In this context, the slow pace was not only about manufacturing speed but also applied to the great time and care taken for procuring material. MANI's workshop undertook the ideas by incorporating naturally dyed organic fabrics produced by traditional Korean methods, high-quality cotton imported from fair-trade organizations in Nepal, or environmentally friendly materials, such as recycled and biodegradable corn-based fabrics from Japan. In this way, MANI's profit model connected Korean garment workers with new transnational civil and consumer subjects, moving away from the current global supply chain of garment manufacturing.

The premise of slowness entailed two tasks: garment making should be temporally organized to make the process slow and humane; and the end product needed to be artisan level. Through these tasks, garment workers would be transformed into artisans. The turn from a unionized action to social enterprise would alleviate the image of militant struggles. While the evolution of Dongdaemun and its fast fashion aggravated what MANI views as a labor problem, the market's survival in the city and its fame helped MANI to develop its place-based cultural politics of activism. Meanwhile, as this chapter continues to explore, the project involved varied institutions and individuals, whose practices complicated the way slowness is imagined and acted on.

Fast Money for a Slow Market

MANI's project gained new momentum by actively participating in the state-sponsored program of social entrepreneurship that emerged around the time, as many other relevant organizations did. However, at the same time, the funding program set out a contradictory financial frame in which MANI had to speed up its project to slow down the pace of work. This irony is embedded in the genealogy of social enterprise, in which the neoliberal transformation of the South Korean social service sector privatized the unemployment problem and took a leading role in developing social enterprises as a new solution.

The social enterprise emerged against a backdrop of the aftermath of the 2008 financial crisis that made a strong impact on Korean society as it did across the globe, especially as to the very idea of "economy" is imagined and discussed. Progressive scholars and activists in South Korea criticized the failure and the contradiction of global capitalism but also were working to recover the "social" in the "economy." New publications, workshops at civil organizations, and special lecture series were concerned with topics such as "thinking Karl Polanyi," "re-reading Marcel Mauss," "the good economy," "humane market in the age of emergency," or the "dead end of capitalism."[5] The anthropologists Mun Young Cho and Seung Chul Lee (2017, 113) analyzed the proliferation of the idea of "the social" in the late 2000s and claimed that it reflected the new hybrid space of cogovernance in which government-led initiatives actively incorporated existing civil actors and the market sector in Korea. Social enterprise (*sahoejeok gieop*) emerged as one of the prime constituencies materializing this cogovernance. Burgeoning research and discussions about ethical consumer movements and new social reformations positioned social enterprise at the intersection of the social and the economic, social welfare and entrepreneurship.

The social welfare policy directly addressed job creation. In the beginning, MANI's small workshop partnered with factories in the area and received funds from the Ministry of Labor's social employment program (*sahoejeok iljari*) to run its classes. Launched in 2003, the social employment program originally aimed to improve the unemployment rate and the poor social services of South Korea, problems that characterized the aftermath of the Asian currency crisis in 1997. While South Korea was known to have rapidly and successfully recovered from the economic collapse and a tough bailout package from the International Monetary Fund that closed large-scale banks and industrial companies, unemployment due to massive layoffs and reduced social services remained as problems. While the unemployment rate itself was not high at the time of my fieldwork, compared to other OECD countries, the average poor quality of jobs were raised as a more distinct problem. First, the portion of daily and temporary workers took up a high portion of (at 45 percent) of all salaried workers with much lower remuneration. Second, the portion of nonsalaried workers, such as self-employed and unpaid family workers, accounted for some 30 percent of the total employment in South Korea (Bidet and Eom 2011). And manufacturing jobs such as garment making took up a significant portion of the lower end of this category. Through the state's social employment program, the government tried to incubate self-supporting social service businesses by creating jobs with public funds. The plan was to financially support companies in the social service fields of welfare, environment, culture, and local development because they were thought to hire marginal individuals, such as low-income individuals, seniors, disabled workers, former sex workers, the homeless, North Korean refugees, single mothers, marriage migrants, and single parents. Garment workers were applicable, having an occupation typically thought of as "low-income." MANI received seed funds to participate in this program by collaborating with local factories that were willing to hire stitching workers who were trained in MANI. However, the program was unsustainable as it structurally led the recipient company to solely depend on the government fund.

In 2006, the Korean government changed the policy focus from social employment to social enterprise. The government enacted the Social Enterprise Promotion Act and instituted the Korea Social Enterprise Promotion Agency in 2010, drawing numerous organizations to participate with innovative projects and creating a "social enterprise boom." Through these acts, the government operated as the primary actor, instituting the new economy and controlling which organization could be officially certified a "social enterprise." This certificate system has been used as a major framework for the general understanding of the investment and management of social enterprise. Even though it is difficult to meet the government's criteria, in January 2010, 7,228 people worked in 251 social enterprises;[6] and the number of new companies registering as social enterprises continued to increase and reached 1,526 companies in 2016.[7]

Local researchers and experts I encountered pointed out that such an evolution was fast, as it was in line with the traditional top-down nature of the developmental regime of the South Korean economy. Just as during the five-year economic developmental plannings of the 1960s and 1980s, the state mobilized vast amounts of investment and led the market to expand, imposed rules that make the market and other actors center on the state institution, and then quickly moved on. Many of my informants compared this swift expansion with the proliferation of "venture enterprises"[8] from 1997 to 2002 using state funds. The anthropologist Jae Chung (2003) commented on this explosive development and quick demise of venture capitalism as "celerity" and conceptualized it as the capitalist logic and the cultural tempo of modern South Korea. Indeed, reports show that South Korea's social enterprise program developed in less than fifteen years, when it had taken some European countries thirty years (Bidet and Eum 2011, 74–80).

While quick seed money for start-up social enterprises offered an immediate opportunity to expand projects and created new possibilities for the future, the fast expansion at the beginning posited a contradiction to its original goal for the slow transformation of the artisan workers. Certified social enterprises are required to launch their own profit-making plan after the initial three years, but sustainability remained a question for most of the model cases, including MANI's enterprise. The three-year funding cycle did not really allow enough time for participants to get trained and become productive to make the profit margin.

This short-paced and frequent budgeting cycle stood in contradiction to MANI's desire to materialize a slower-paced work life in the harsh market environment. Even when the skills of the participants were not yet fully matured, MANI created a production line to hire more. It was required criteria to show how much the given enterprise *reinvested* the return to social values (i.e., hiring a person of marginal position). Yet MANI members took it as an integral task to keep up with renewing the funding cycle and applying for new funding sources, while changing their organizational structure, when necessary. The ongoing project was supposed to be material evidence that the proposed future was struggling but certainly on the way.

In addition to the state funds, MANI also drew funds from investment bankers and large corporations, who started to see the social enterprise as a useful public sector for corporate participation. As a result, MANI continuously faced multiple budget cycles. The three-year pilot project that shaped MANI was funded through a combination of state funds and other financial resources.[9] While the contract between MANI and the government was for three years, the report and review took place twice a year. The result of this assessment framed the yearly budget cycle and determined the continuation of the project period. In each report, MANI had to offer an extensive analysis of the review from participants and the enterprise's degree of success in helping participants advance their skills and find a better job. MANI staff members felt that they were prone to criticism in this yearly review because there was not much "achievement," conceived of as participants with tangible promotions or new jobs. Achievement has become an important issue for the staff members in every budget cycle, collecting the survey responses, facing unsatisfactory feedback from the participants, and writing up reports explaining the tangible achievements.

Immoral Speed and Embodied Paces of Work

While the bureaucratic and financial cycle pressed for a tangible result within a short time, controlling the tempo of work proved to be a challenging task. MANI's sewing skill classes and the Company aimed to slow down the pace of work in pursuit of recovering connections between garment makers, their labor, and their products. Workers were introduced to the entire process of garment production, from fabric cutting and finishing to creating complex designs and delicate fabrics. Yet slow pace was a subjective concept and hard to standardize. Moreover, the pace of work that participants embody (earned through decades of work) revealed the contradictions and ambiguities in MANI's vision.

During the sewing skills enhancement class, when someone's sewing machine made a loud and aggressive motorized sound, the instructor mocked, "Who is the one pushing numbers [Nuga jangsu ppopgo isseo]?"—pointing out that the person was rushing the machine and insinuating that the person was working only for quantity, not quality. The culprits would often exchange sheepish smiles with their classmates. Speed signified the urge to make money, with little attention to the quality of the product and the quality of the worker's life. Speed also signified low-level garment making, characterized by a mass-produced product lacking quality and originality. The machine would make a softer sound if one uses it with care. The instructor and MANI staff continuously emphasized to the participants that artisan techniques were not geared toward how fast a person could work but the quality of clothes that one could produce; fast work was associated with mindless labor.

However, "proper pace" was often unclear due to the slippage between blind speed, high-level sewing skills, productivity, and the quality of the end product. The subtle line between speed of work, the level of finished quality, and the empowerment of the workers was even more ambiguous at the Company, where participants should have been integrated as highly skilled artisan workers. Unlike the sewing class, in the social enterprise the outcome needed to meet a "productive efficiency" standard, which included standardized quality, designated due dates and quantity, and a social and liberating work environment. It was not desirable to work "too slowly" as one would do for made-to-order clothes, art craft, or amateur clothes. Several workshop participants told me that to produce "high-end-level" quality of ready-made clothes, one could only practice and constantly adjust to the efficient speed and to the quality of the work. The seam is straight and clean only when the sewing machine is working at a certain speed. A gracefully sounding motor was a tangible sign of the "right" speed, although this marker was ambiguous.

The biggest challenge seemed to be unlearning the work pace that the participants had embodied throughout their entire career. Many of the people working in the Company used to work in the ordinary ready-made apparel factories and outsourcing factories and were not accustomed to doing the highly structured line work to meet a standardized quality or to the delicate collaborative work of making formal clothing with natural dyes. Rather, many workers were accustomed to doing their own work at their own pace, assembling and stitching the entire garment. Misun, who led the line production, explained how MANI staff promoted a slow pace of work by encouraging the women to talk with each other about their work and to synchronize their work rhythms with each other. However, some participants found this method upsetting because they felt it infringed on the independence of their own pace of work. Additionally, the work style at MANI that allowed time for socializing among the workers did not necessarily empower the workers. Even Misun acknowledged problems with this working style, suggesting that seams become loose once you lose "the consistency and repetitive rhythm [of sewing]," by which she meant that once you begin sewing a seam, you should not stop in the middle. Accidents [*sago*], mainly caused by glitches in the assembly line, would also occur, disrupting their sense of control over work.

Like fastness, slowness is not neutral. Controlled paces, whether sped up or slowed down, and the very idea of controlling the pace of work, put pressure and create confusion for those who perform and embody a particular pace of work. The imposed slowness and the glitches revealed not only the longtime disciplined body for the pressure for sped-up production but also the attachments, keen awareness, and subjective senses of performance that people have developed over years of their work.

Enduring Support: Memories and Indebtedness to the Past

While MANI's project stays in progress, it has been surrounded by a retrospective sense of affection and obligation for the heyday of social activism during the

1960s–1980s in Dongdaemun. During this period, as I also illustrate in chapter 5, garment labor played a pivotal role in leading the broader social and democratization movement. In retrospect, the garment labor and activism are central to what people remember about the past and the way they engage with the labor movement and the problem of the authoritarian state and dictatorship. MANI crystallized these memories as the best time of garment manufacturing, the worst time of labor exploitation, and the most rigorous time for labor activism. MANI drew social, ethical, and sometimes monetary support from those who have these memories and emotional investments.

When I first started working at MANI, I was mainly engaged in clerical work, including translating English materials into Korean, making photocopies, and editing documents. After a few weeks, I was asked to digitize MANI's entire contact list. Working for three full days, I encountered the organizations' vast network. It included not only other social activist groups but also various members of trade associations, media groups, large corporations, politicians, and academics. For MANI's projects and events, such as the annual workshop and the social enterprise, the organization worked in collaboration with large corporations and collective labor unions, although they did not seem very compatible with MANI in a conventional sense.

Although MANI still grappled with the tensions and pressure to sustain its projects, it continuously drew attention and support from the personal networks of those who remembered the past and dreamed of making a significant social change. Yoonsung, a journalist whom I met in a reading group, was one of them. Yoonsung knew some participants in the MANI project and wrote an article on the project in the newspaper she used to work for. Like numerous other people I encountered in Korea, Yoonsung had been involved in labor activism and social reformation during the 1980s and was well informed about MANI. Even though Yoonsung and others had different takes on MANI's project and goals, they all acknowledged the symbolic significance of garment labor activism in Korean society. The year 2010 marked the fortieth anniversary of Taeil Chun's death, the legendary labor activist and fabric cutter in Pyeoghwa Market in Dongdaemun; numerous roundtable discussions, rituals, and events took place to commemorate the event.[10] Yoonsung commented on the garment workers: "I bet [MANI] has shortcomings and internal problems as do all other social movements, but it is impressive that they keep getting funds while others do not. I also personally admire that they came this far in the 2000s. I think that Korean society has a sense of indebtedness [buchaeuisik] to the 1970s and 1980s for what happened back then. Who would dare turn their back on the legacy of Chun Taeil, honestly?"

Yoonsung's use of the word buchae was engrained in the context of the labor and democratization movement in South Korea. Used as a more formal word for *bit* (debt), *buchae* colloquially refers both to a debt and to a moral obligation.[11] The word also reflects Yoonsung's sentiment of the generation who were actively involved in the student protest and democratization movement.[12] I heard similar stories from other participants who joined MANI, thinking about their former coworkers or their own old days. The term describes the complex sense of contriteness for those who feel that they did not participate enough and that the stability and prosperity they experience today is due to the sacrifice and passion of others.

Multiple organizations and social enterprises related to the garment industry claim to uphold the "spirit of Chun" (Chun Taeil *jeongsin*). However, quite a few social activists I met around MANI mentioned that "the field" (*hyeonjang*), or the field of action or praxis for collective movements, had radically changed: workshops were dispersed, and workers became mostly independent subcontractors (S. Park 2019b). The collective bargaining of wage and working hours also lost its power in the intensifying supply chain system. The home-factories that chapter 2 discussed also were viewed as fragmented sites that disable proper mobilization. For some activists who saw this as desperation, MANI reenergized and revamped the labor movement, and the legendary garment labor unions comprised MANI's network in various ways. MANI's advocacy for "clothes made by Korean labor" appealed to the uniform market, including uniforms for schools, hospitals, and civil organizations. The progressive teachers' association and other manufacturing labor unions were responsive to MANI's suggestion that students are the future of Korea and that those who care about Korean laborers should wear uniforms produced in Korea in a nonexploitative manner.

This sense of baggage and responsibility is not merely a revival of the past form of activism and contestation but leads to a different terrain of investment for social change. Jesook Song's (2009) ethnographic inquiry into the welfare society of South Korea analyzes the participation of former social activists in the contemporary neoliberal welfare society and suggests this creates a dilemma in South Korean intellectual history. MANI's project could be seen in a similar vein, in that former social activists attempt to solve the unemployment and class problems within the market logic, in this case, the model of social enterprise. As the involvement of Yoonsung and others demonstrates, the state funding agency, social enterprise program, labor activism, and the workshop are performed and connected by individuals who have moral and affective connection to each other and to their previous investment and responsibility in labor activism.[13] For these figures, the formal success of the social enterprise within the structure of the government's funding programs or the promotion of the participants in the higher position matters less than keeping past networks and ideals intact. As Song suggests, the different trajectories complicate the new spaces of labor and market movements and, furthermore, link them through projects like MANI's.

Even those who do not have direct connections to garment manufacturing see the symbolic meaning that the industry represents. Younghye quit her job as a chief designer in a major apparel company of Korea, where she had worked for twenty years, to serve as a designer at MANI. Younghye explained that her fatigue toward her previous work as a designer paralleled her skepticism toward the "knowledge workers" whom she encountered around the fashion and garment industry as well as intellectual-activists of other sectors. Participating in MANI provided her with a feeling of being closer to "the very basic origin of what I have been working on." The materiality of garment manufacturing and its symbolic presence in Korean modern history incited personal investment in social reformation, such as MANI, providing resources and moral support. For those who have moral or nostalgic attachments to garment manufacturing, like Yoonsung or Younghye, Dongdaemun remained a significant symbolic place where one could see and feel the presence of others making clothes and the historical memories of the industrial labor of the 1960s and 1980s. Rather than the radical change or swift funding that government sponsorship might bring out, it was these retrospective investments that prolonged and sustained the life of MANI.

Shared Hopes, Dissident Paths

While MANI's projects carried multiple and contradictory forces in pushing its goal to slow down labor, it often invited various figures who express strong interest in and passion for garment work. As a countermirror of the market, MANI became an outlet for narratives that would otherwise have not been visible.

The activists, factory owners, and garment workers I encountered during fieldwork (particularly at MANI) were concerned about the lack of younger workers in the garment manufacturing scene. Previous chapters have discussed how garment work in Korea is marginalized as temporally obsolete and relegated to a South Korean economy of the past. While MANI addressed moral and economic responsibility toward experienced workers, staff members also tried to find a way to bring "vitality" to the manufacturing scene and to represent sewing skills as something that would attract the younger generation. Incorporating younger generations into garment manufacturing appeared to be an important goal for the fundamental premise of social enterprise as creating jobs for the currently productive population and training them in a new skill. Despite the contradiction of hasty funding sources that required quick proof of tangible accomplishments, the hope was that these young workers would benefit from the training class, find the right career path, or even join the Company.

However, participants did not always fit neatly into the categories of desirable workers delineated by MANI. The free sewing class series offered by MANI attracted many individuals with unexpected profiles, who had various connections to sewing and a dream of "making clothes." Some had been working in Dongdaemun and came back after a long absence; others were middle-class housewives who came to learn sewing in this fully subsidized class; still others had very rudimentary sewing skills and vague hopes of making clothes. While many people's motivations and goals did not always fit MANI's plan for labor revitalization, their attachment to and passion for their work and affect for each other nonetheless mobilized them and many others within the market.

Sunghye, a successful MANI graduate, became a symbolic figure for two semesters in MANI. College educated, Sunghye learned fast. Starting in the beginner's class, Sunghye was invited to the sewing skills class for the second half and was then hired by the Company as a stitching assistant. Sunghye used to work in her fiancé's wholesale store, which inspired her to sell clothes that she designed. The desire to be a good designer led her to MANI's workshop. Sunghye had the virtue of a young body, acquired new skills quickly, was flexible in the environment, and was willing to go through the long, tedious process of apprenticing as a seamstress to apply it to creative designing. MANI did not want to lose her, so they accelerated her training, even providing her with a scholarship. But despite her success within the program, Sunghye had reservations about the spotlight she received:

> I know the activists and staff are skeptical about the wholesale market and traders, but to me it is not that different, in the sense that I deal with clothes anyway. Since I have seen great failure in selling clothes, this social enterprise also seems very risky to me. I had sold clothes and made 28 million won [approximately $25,000] in two days during one weekend, when the marketplace was going really well. I saw some successful stores across from us make 30 million won [approximately $27,500] in one night. Now the clothes, money, and people have faded away. . . . One good thing is that, after the hype is gone, now my partner and my friends understand why I want to be on the other side [of making clothes].

Her fiancé and friends teased Sunghye for *choosing* to become a "twenty-first-century factory girl" (*21segi gongsuni*), which to them seemed like an unlikely choice for a Korean woman in her thirties. Through mockery, her counterparts expressed concern that Sunghye would not make it through the long hours of manual labor. And yet despite her friends' concerns, she did not see making and selling clothes as simply oppositional, and she was able to jump into the training for stitching. Only occasionally have there been young women like Sunghye who endeavor to learn sewing skills. The aging of garment labor and the industry itself was a greater barrier to getting young people to enter in the field than economic devaluation (S. Park 2019a). While she was aware of the big gap between her own experiences and the older participants' lives, Sunghye still saw continuity between herself and them based on their shared engagement with clothes. This experience resonated with the experiences of other women introduced in previous chapters who often crossed the domains of designing, manufacturing, and trading through their lives and their networks, despite the discursive division and hierarchy between the domains of work.

I was also struck by the continuity that a participant like Sunghye saw between the market and the countermarket. As Sunghye noted in the quote above, MANI and Dongdaemun did not stand in opposition as both markets are operating fast and are risky speculations. Yet she wanted to pursue work in which she could "sit and deal with the clothes," get enough money to feed herself, and receive a decent income at the end of every day. Dongdaemun is where clothes are always made and sold, even to a modest degree. For her, MANI's project was not an alternative or in opposition to Dongdaemun but rather a better or different reentry point to Dongdaemun.

Sunghye's classmate Midong talked about a similar desire. After one semester, the whole class went to a workshop in Goesan, a small county in Chungcheongbuk-do. The two-day workshop was designed to be an annual self-review for MANI staff and participants. As participants chatted after dinner, Midong's unusual past drew attention. A sixty-year-old woman, Midong used to be a ceramic artist. She majored in pottery and ceramics in college and used to be a professional pottery maker with her own kiln in Icheon, a town near Seoul known for its famous community of pottery artists, galleries, and private kilns.

For the first time since we met, Midong revealed how she had become involved with MANI. The staff had rejected her application two times over the past two years. They told Midong that she seemed not a good fit for their project. Given limited seats and resources funded by the government's assistance and donations, MANI staff were reluctant to accept unusual participants like Midong, who did not seem to be desperate to survive in the garment-making field. Their doubts were straightforward: Why would a pottery artist with a college degree and an extensive portfolio want to become a garment worker? They added that it also seemed a bit late for her to start learning to sew. The staff initially recommended that she take a garment alteration course instead of intensive stitching training courses. Midong confronted the staff, saying that she wanted to upgrade her sewing skills to be able to make a career of them, not just to enjoy as a hobby. In contrast to the staff's judgment, Midong claimed that she was motivated to learn sewing precisely because she was sixty years old, not younger. At this age, Midong had started to have a different perspective on work and realized what is important in one's work. Midong finally earned a spot in the class and enthusiastically participated in the class after her part-time work at a supermarket.

While there were health and financial reasons in the decision Midong made to leave her kiln, Midong said she felt that she was not surviving in the pottery market and the competitive world as an artist. According to Midong, pottery making is a lot like sewing; both skills are acquired through an extensive period of apprenticeship, and both are conducted in harsh working environments. However, according to Midong, the difference was that potters rely on the free labor of trainees and their families, especially their wives. She said:

> Doing simple jobs, such as molding the clay and carrying the pots, does not make one an artist. You basically need those who are doing the work for you, and then you earn a reputation as an artist. Those who are doing the other work won't be considered artists. Ceramic art sometimes comes from a random chance, but so many other mediocre ones come about as well. For that tedious part, you rely on your wife, apprentice, and many others. For twenty years I was doing this simple repetitive job myself, feeling like I was just manufacturing ready-made pots with an empty name [of artist].

Midong said that what bothered her most was not having to do the repetitive work but having to deal with being called an artist, which she felt did not appropriately describe the work she did in her day-to-day life. At least in the small group discussion, participants from different occupations, even the experienced seamstresses who were leading the sewing class, seemed to be convinced by her self-reflective analysis about her work. Midong said,

> It is very hard to distinguish who really has "good" skills and artistry. Without the free labor of your wife and apprentices, potters cannot make enough money and also cannot represent themselves as artisans. There were times when the Japanese buyers were crazy about Korean pottery and would come to buy even the failed stuff rolled out from the kiln. . . . But these things are not sustainable. I kilned day and night and just could not compete with the so-called artisans who have more manpower. Finally, only recently, I realized that I want to have basic skills that are not ostentatious but raw. I want an immediate relationship with what I make, a connection [with my work] without barrier.

The contrast between Midong and Sunghye illuminates what MANI's counter-market project shares with the market itself. Sunghye and Midong look radically different considering their time of life—their age, their stage of life, and possible changes in their living conditions. And their "fit" for MANI's project was in contrast as well. For the slower production, Sunghye's flexibility and youth could make a fast accomplishment and expedite the future prospect of a creative artisan with high-quality sewing skills. Midong's stubborn body would find it hard to adjust. However, their narratives echoed a similar attachment to and passion for the work, work that connects one immediately with the materiality of clothes. In their utterly realistic vision, creative work is never guaranteed by having a college degree, being young, or having artistry in their work. Altering the pace of work and idealized work schedule do not directly enhance or transform the conditions of life and labor.

However, the seemingly anachronistic pursuits of sewing skills of Midong and Sunghye for a better work future challenged the discursive devaluation of garment work that many current workers have taken for granted. The border between art craft and commodity manufacturing is distinctive but also a matter for subjective understanding. As the conversation afterward proceeded, the group started to talk about motivations they have about various registers of garment work, from designing, stitching, reforming, alterations, and even applying needlework to producing different kinds of fabric goods. Everybody was excited to hear about two old seamstresses in their seventies who were apparently working in the garment factories in Seoul and Ilsan. In the conversation, participants shared their sense of attachment to work in a variety of ways, including their desire to perform work that a woman can do autonomously, pride in mastering sewing skills, and appreciation of making something tangible and material in life. Similar conversations happened numerous times at MANI, in one of which Sanghee shared her story about designing new items in her stitching factory, as discussed in chapter 3. While the ideal of "artisanal stitcher" did not pertain to Sanghee's case, her excitement reminded other seamstresses of similar experiences and decision they made in the past and inspired others to take pride in their work, as well. For the participants in this diverse range, including foreign migrant women, old women who were seeking a new skill and job opportunity, young designers like Sunghye, or old artists like Midong, these common threads unfolded in the women's personal narratives of work in life.

Conclusion

MANI's project shows how the critique of speed has become a local discursive issue that converges with a sense of crisis for manufacturing industrial workers and activists facing deindustrialization and an emerging historical awareness about South

Korea's rapid industrial growth in the past. The project also shows the complex intersection of dissident institutions and economic regimes: labor activism, ethical consumerism, social enterprise, and the neoliberal welfare state. The project has been simultaneously driven and stalled by its heterogeneous paces, short-term budget cycles of the state and corporate funds that required evidence of impossibly rapid achievement, emotional reluctance and elongated support of labor activists toward these swift transformations, the moral problematization of the production speed, and the fast-paced work that the workers have embodied over thirty years of work. The disjunctures between and among them manifest in the incongruent temporalities of the everyday practice of this experimental space that MANI has created. Understanding these layers of investments and practices helps us to see how an organization like MANI opens up a social setting through which variously positioned actors participate in altering and reproducing the market and also multiple paces and tracks of time in the market itself.

Meanwhile, MANI's project reveals and reminds us of the critical aspects of the problem of speed that this book has engaged with. The arbitrary and ambiguous connection between the speed at work, the quality of the finished product, and the empowerment and experiences of the workers evinces the difficulty of the singular politics of labor and time. Going back to Jonghee's anxiety, introduced at the beginning of this chapter, the social enterprise project did meet a success in a near future. The new tempos for artisanship were not fully developed among the workers due to the entanglement of their aging and naturally slowing body, embodied pace of work, and sense of work they have developed through the sped-up production and circulation. It is not that the sped-up work served as an innate and intact problem to the workers themselves but that the sped-up paces of work, even problematic and exploitative, has done *more* than just the shortened cycle of production for the workers themselves. As much as their decades-long experiences and memories have been the major target of MANI's advocacy and a major source of branding its project, these experiences and memories have developed with their embodied paces of work, the social relations around them, and the sense of mastery of their own skills and productivity, all of which the first three sections of this book have endeavored to show. MANI's intervention in commodity production was based on the same basic assumption in capitalist logic—that speed is external to the body and can be controlled and commanded. This shared assumption would constantly be incompatible with the embodied and experienced paces of work. The imposed and engineered slowness, which needed to be expedited for the success of the project, would remain discordant with the naturally slowing and aging body of Jonghee.

Tangible accomplishment, rather, came from those spontaneous moments within the project in which participants with differing backgrounds bring together their accounts of motivation and the self-interpretation of the value of work. Throughout my fieldwork, there were numerous conversations in and out of the organization's program, intentionally and unintentionally, where new articulations of past and future work could be narrated and shared. Even though MANI itself did not become the future for them, the space it opened shifted the image of garment work from a dominant frame that denigrated garment labor as cheap, repetitive, victimized, and no longer relevant to the South Korean economy, to a more diverse and flexible field of work that is worthwhile to invest one's life and alternate future in.

PACING THE FLOW

During our interview, Oksun, serving as one of MANI's leading seamstress, was describing a typical get-together in Dongdaemun with her friends Eunju and Sumi. All in their fifties, the three friends used to actively participate in labor activism in the 1970s and 1980s and spent their late teens and twenties together. Their paths have diverged after the rigor of activism with the Cheonggye Labor Union. Yet, for these women in their fifties, Dongdaemun has been a default location for meeting up, as it is centrally located with convenient access to transportation and also as they are all quite familiar with the place. From adjacent neighborhoods with factories, to garment wholesale plazas that used to be factories, to the streets that weave throughout the area, every corner of Dongdaemun carried the trajectories and memories of these women.

The three friends met up at a subway station and strolled down pedestrian paths along the Cheonggye stream, the eleven-kilometer-long modern waterway that runs through Dongdaemun and downtown Seoul. The original stream that flowed through Seoul during the Joseon dynasty (1392–1910) was first partially covered during the period of Japanese colonial rule (1910–1945). The urban planning project put into effect after the Korean War (1950–51) completed the paving of the stream and built a highway on the top of it. This overpass cuts across Seoul from east to west, enabling a fast connection between the inner city and the rest of the country. Cheonggyecheon streets, below the Cheonggye overpass, were a primary corridor around which Dongdaemun's sweatshops and warehouses clustered from the 1960s to the 1980s, as many of my interlocutors remember. The dark, shadowy streets served as a primary symbol of arduous manual labor and activism.

Now the Cheonggyecheon area is bright and open, after the massive restoration project in 2003 removed the elevated highway and revived the urban stream. Along the abundant eleven-kilometer-long water flow, riverbanks are well kept, verdant with short bushes and trees. Pedestrian boardwalks became one of the most popular attractions, inviting new cafés, hotels, and high-rise office buildings in adjacent areas. Once a town of laborers and garment sellers, metal tools, and machines industry, the area now is also crowded with foreign tourists, shoppers, and passersby in suits commuting to their business offices. The spectacle of the long water channel in the heart of the city has become one of the most prominent landmarks of Seoul, radically transforming the inner-city landscape over the past fifteen years.

The three friends would walk up to the Chun Taeil Bridge, one of the twenty-two pedestrian bridges spanning the stream. The bridge is near Cheonggyecheon 6th Street, where many major factories used to be located, and Pyeonghwa Market mall, one of the oldest malls in the Dongdaemun area. It was also a spot where Chun Taeil set himself on fire in 1970 in protest of the authoritarian government and garment companies. As second-generation labor activists, young laborers who emerged after Chun's death, the three friends had once been taken to the spot of his legendary suicide, where burn marks were still visible on the concrete street. Thirty years later, on the bridge, they can now view his statue (figure 5.2) and bronze plaques (figure 5.1) dedicated to the garment manufacturing and labor movements. The three friends' names were inscribed on the plaques, as they had made small donations to the construction project (figure 5.1), beside many other public figures, including previous presidents Kim Yeong-sam, Kim Dae-jung, and Roh Moo-hyun, as well as current and former labor and democratization movement activists. Oksun commented on her plaque: "I am proud that our life trajectory is inscribed on the bridge, but the bridge and the Chun Taeil statue seem *out of place*. . . . It just happened so quickly, and I am not really sure what to feel about it."

Oksun's phrase "out of place" conveys both spatial and temporal senses. Connecting the wholesale stores that sell clothes, fabrics, and materials, the bridges carry traffic still predominantly consisting of bike couriers, workers, and vendors for garment, metal, or electric manufacturing and wholesaling, whose population has dropped in recent years. More importantly, Oksun's comment suggests that the history of the garment industry and activism memorialized in this bridge stand out and do not blend with other parts of the area. The dominant discourse of the restoration project celebrated the excavation of the remnants of the Joseon dynasty, the revival of ancient and original nature, and the bright future of this eco-friendly city.

Gradually, I came to understand that the sense of (in)adequacy is not merely about the landscape but more deeply intertwined with her own trajectories as a garment worker and an activist. While in previous chapters, we encountered the city space of Dongdaemun as an active presence in the shaping of the temporal

FIGURE 5.1. Bronze dedication plaques set into the pavement of the bridge. Inscribed are the names of organizations and individuals who donated money for the commemorative bridge. Quick-service delivery motorbikes are seen behind.

Photo by the author.

meanings and politics of work, this chapter examines the city's longer span of time to show my interlocutors' historical awareness as it is shaped their engagement with their lives and labor.

Continuing the discussion of chapter 4, I suggest that it is not only the emphasis on actual rapidity but also the way the rapidity has been problematized

FIGURE 5.2.   Chun Taeil's statue

Photo by the author.

that shapes the temporality of the city. The urban developmentalism of South Korea particularly posits the problem of the sped-up city as something of the "past"—the period of "ugly modernization" from the 1960s to the 1980s. This linear frame of history brought to the forefront a rupture from the past in the current planning project and gave moral and temporal value to the restored stream as "new," "future-oriented," "civil," and "humane." What made it new, however, was city planning's representation of the fast-paced city as a problematic legacy of the past, rather than the actual execution of the transformation. While the three friends' shared experiences as factory women posits them as figures of the past, their persistent presence in the space and their narratives destabilize the neatly packaged landscape and the unilinear history it inscribes in the space.

This chapter takes the Cheonggyecheon stream as a starting point to think through contestations over the linear passage of history, which I conceptualize as a problem of flow. I use the term "flow" as a metaphor to highlight the actual and imagined fluvial motion of the stream itself, the passage of time from past to present, and the mobility of lives, vehicles, and the capital. As Matthew Gandy (2014, 8) illustrates in *The Fabric of Space*, water lies at the intersection of landscape and infrastructure, crossing between visible and invisible domains of urban space, and unsettles our existing conceptions of space, technology, and landscape. In this chapter, the flow is an actual and conceptual space that is particularly temporalized—the aquatic environment that is electronically pumped to move regularly and straightforwardly, the mobility of commodities in rapid production and circulation, and the imagined passage of the urban and social history of Dongdaemun and broader Seoul. As much as the stream's actual fluvial movement is the primary spectacle of the current landscape, the idea of pacing up or slowing down the flow of material production and circulation manifests in the languages of urban planning and in their critiques.

Through analyzing these complex layers, I argue that the efforts to control the flow of people, vehicles, and commodities and to create a new path for labor and urban politics eventually reveal more complexities and incongruent tempos, cycles, and paces within the flows. The narratives and paths of working bodies, components of the flow itself, challenge the linear notion of the history of the city. Subsequent sections start from a larger flow: the irony of the rapid urban planning projects of this area. The recent urban projects in 2000 claimed a shift from the rapidity of urban flow from the 1960s to the 1980s and aspired to rebrand the city with a slower pace of nature, pedestrian, and the postindustrial economy. This promise and the desire for the "new flow," however, justified the expedited rendition and the brutality of the sped-up planning project that transformed the built environment. Then, the chapter zooms into Chun Taeil Bridge to discuss its more nuanced role to materialize and open a space of commemoration, both supporting and complicating the new flow that the urban planning projects desire to create. Lastly, it takes a closer look at the three friends' narratives and discusses the way they make sense of their own trajectories and carve out a path that unsettles the singular notion of the flow and the singular temporality of urban and labor politics.

Flow to the Future, Straight Lines

Paving over Cheonggyecheon stream and Dongdaemun's development parallel one another as icons of the rapid urbanization and industrialization of Seoul. Bokkyu Yum (2015), an urban historian of modern Korea, suggested that the paving of Cheonggyecheon stream and the construction of the Cheonggye overpass made the area an ultimate "1960s' space [*1960nyeondae-jeok Gonggan*]," characterized by a radical rupture from the colonial past, led by the complicit interplay of state power and the capital.

The paving of Cheonggyecheon stream and the construction of the highway overpass were driven by the same motivations that Neferti Tadiar (2004) observed in the case of flyover constructions and the state-led urban economy of Manila. According to Tadiar (2004, 88–89), an overpass serves as both an *expression and*

reminds me of the steel factories

instrument of urban desire for the "unhindered and unhampered flow" of capital and national prosperity. And this desired flow could only be obtained by controlling the "excess" of undesired people and traffic.[1] From the growth-centered, urban-development planning perspective, covering up the stream would transform the area from an urban ghetto into a "productive" space by cleaning out undesirable elements, including waste, smell, and the urban poor. The development plan solved the problems of sanitation and the stench that came from the sewage that flowed into the Cheonggyecheon by filling it in with concrete and constructing a vehicle-centered road system that also drove out the underprivileged residents of the space, including beggars, orphans, and homeless people. The overpass led to the growth of mass garment manufacturing in Dongdaemun by efficiently routing trucks and long-distance buses through the district, enabling it to become a hub of cheap garment manufacturing and wholesale marketing. Since then, the dark streets under the overpass, from Cheonggyecheon 1st to 9th Streets, with the "excess" population working in warehouses, small workshops, and wholesale stores, have supported the rapid growth of Seoul as a city based on manufacturing industrialization.

In the 1990s, however, the flow channeled and amplified on the overpass came to be excessively jammed, and the overpass itself started to look dark and old. Originally built as a clean, effective, and modern urban infrastructure, the growth of the city brought traffic and congestion to the overpass and the surrounding area. The decay was not merely about functionality. Cheonggye overpass's constant congestion and stalled traffic flow revealed the increasing imbalance and failure to control the excess—the unwanted presence of labor, commodities, and vehicles for dwindling manufacturing industry. Critics blamed this urban blight (and others, such as environmental pollution, labor exploitation, and ghettoization) on the developmentalist growth of Seoul from the 1960s to the 1980s, and broadly, cast Cheonggyecheon as the epitome of the urban problems of this period.

In 2003, when then-mayor Lee Myung-bak began ambitiously proposing a radically new flow of water through the Cheonggyecheon restoration project, he actively made use of this signification and posited the project as an innovative experiment and notable rupture from past state-led development, which arguably won him the presidential election in 2008. Hong Kal (2011) points out that the restoration project's image of an "open stream [and] green future" cannot be separated from Lee's career as a leading figure of growth-centered urban development during the 1960s–1980s. Indeed, the massive-scale restoration project only took a little more than two years. An equally massive scale of discontents followed, from the dislocated vendors and manufacturers,[2] historians and activists who were frustrated by the way existing and newly excavated historical artifacts were violated and mistreated, and environmentalists and urban engineers who questioned the efficacy and sustainability of the waterway. Yet none of them made a significant impact in slowing down the process. Lee (2007) boldly touted his "know-how" in pushing forward the planning project in his monograph, *Cheong-gyecheon Flows to Future*. He was also often covered in the international media for turning his urban-planning experience toward championing the idea of "green growth" (Bina 2013).[3] This "new developmentalism" often referred to a paradigm shift from a blind pursuit of industry-driven development to one of balanced and sustainable development with greater concern for the environment, livability, and the public good. The case was featured in international media and documentary films as a new trend among Asian megacities[4] and as showing how people can care for urban nature that had been once "lost."[5]

However, the stream's flow is symbolically and virtually entangled with the demolished overpass. The stream follows the line of the overpass, its predecessor, showing an aesthetic parallel, what Seokhoon Woo (2008) calls an "aesthetics of straightness" that he associates with South Korean senses of developmentalism. The fast, uniform flow is controlled by an electric pump, which uses 2,200 kilowatts of electricity and costs $6.7 million per year to operate. The pump brings 120,000 tons of water every day from the Han River and its tributaries, the major water source for Seoul, and groundwater drawn from the downtown subway stations. This water supply literally stops when there is a blackout in the area. Just as the Cheonggye overpass was prone to traffic jams and eventually failed to sustain its "unhindered flow" of traffic and industrial capital, the restored Cheonggyecheon stream also fails to manage its contradictions and imbalances from the sped-up straightness. The new, restored "nature" actually contains more functional, aesthetic, and historical similarities with the demolished "culture," the man-made concrete highway.

Local scholars and critics often have used the term "new developmentalism" (*singaebaljuui*) not to connote the newness of it but to foreground the unchanging nature of old developmentalism and its political ideology. The deconstruction and reconstruction process had persistently been hasty and justified bulldozing the old for the sake of progress. For instance, the urban theorist Myung-Rae Cho (2010, 21–22) sees the Cheonggyecheon restoration as "instrumental environmentalism" and closer to "installation" or "gardening" rather than the real restoration of ecology. According to Cho, the stream symbolizes the tenacious lack of ecological and historical authenticity among the power elites of the state. Jong Youl Lee and Chad David Anderson (2013) criticize the lack of tenant input and unequal distribution of the potential benefits of the project, a lingering problem in Korean urban development. The sociologist Seongtae Hong's insights are particularly notable. Seongtae Hong (2014) unpacks developmentalism itself and argues that developmentalism did not end in the 1960s–1970s but has taken different forms over time. According to Hong (2014, 234–70), this notion of development has been so omnipresent that it makes it difficult for Korean society to separate the sense of progress associated with development from speculative interests that only benefit a few.

This logic of development operated powerfully in Cheonggyecheon as an urban infrastructure. The tightly structured system of renewal, led by the coalition of the state and business conglomerates, has evolved for decades amid what David Harvey (2001) would describe as postindustrial strategies for commodifying space itself rather than constructing the city as a platform for material production (Shin and Kim 2016). Immediately after the completion of the restoration project, the Seoul metropolitan government reported positive responses from citizens and subsequently increased numbers of the visitors.[6] As a public space that connects to the center of the city, there was only a narrow strip of ground for street vendors and workshop workers, who could only tenuously argue for their right to the space without any residency status. The fact that Cheonggyecheon came to operate as a vibrant public sphere in the heart of downtown made it even harder for collective protest or criticism of the result, which eventually obscured the brutality of the hasty deconstruction and reconstruction process. The Cheonggyecheon *gwanjang* (plaza) near the upstream area and open spaces along the riverbank has been often used for diverse campaigns, protests, citizen-led events, school trips to study urban ecology, and so on.

A sense of belonging further complicated the position of criticism. "Would anybody have imagined enjoy walking around here before? It was only depressing and despicable," said Eunju, one of the three friends, offering a positive remark about the restoration project. Eunju added later that it was even a "touching experience" to be able to see the sky from the Cheonggye streets. Eunju was cynical of and critical toward state leadership and policy, especially for working-class laborers, as she was still actively involved in the labor and democratization movement. She had even joined her activist friends supporting the evictees protesting the Dongdaemun Design Plaza (which I will discuss in the following section) before the protesting tents were removed. Yet, as she had invested her earlier life in Cheonggyecheon through her work in factories and activism, it was hard for her to simply renounce the "betterment" that she currently observed. The ambiguous sense of belonging and attachment here was not merely to the current space and its landscape but also to the symbolic history. I will come back to this point.

Flow to the Future, in Streamline

The South Korean state's interest in instituting a creative knowledge economy has made an impact on the way garment stitching labor and design work in Dongdaemun are imagined, represented, and valorized, as discussed earlier in this book in the introduction and chapter 3. The ideal of making a radical rupture from the past form of industry and advance to a new future by means of new forms of knowledge production was a part of the larger planning project Design City, led by then-mayor Oh Se-hoon (2006–2010). Design City posited Seoul's future as a hub of global city networks, the creative economy, and financial capital for speculative development.

The "Design Seoul" project attempted a shift from a "hard city" to a "soft city" that is expected to make the city globally popular and lucrative as a result.[7] The project presented a meticulous guideline that characterized a hard city as "addicted to speed" and centered on construction, industry, function, and efficiency. In contrast, progress to a soft city suggested a slow-paced built environment for pedestrians or bikers and centered on art and culture. The guideline posited that the soft city would render "aesthetic, exciting, humane" qualities to the lives of urbanites, the qualities that had been sacrificed for functionality in the old development style of "rapid growth."[8] Newly instituted regulations on the size and design of signboards for commercial buildings and public facilities brought about a quick change on the facade of the built environment in the city.

This supposedly slow mode that the city would undertake to promote creativity, however, escalated in Dongdaemun with the ambition of rebranding the city as global. The Global City Forum Seoul, an annual forum cosponsored by the city of Seoul, was one of the sites where Oh's office would promote and confirm Seoul's new branding. Numerous "internationally acclaimed scholars" (*segyejeokin seokhak*) in geography, urban studies, and architecture were invited to the forum, which took place four times consecutively during Oh's term. I was able to attend the forum in 2009 as an audience member, as it took place during my extensive fieldwork. "Can Seoul be a global city?" The question, put forth by the mayor himself, was posed multiple times during the forum. During their presentations and floor discussions, the keynote speakers from North America both mentioned Dongdaemun, which they had observed during the organized tour prior to the public meeting, as part of the forum's program for invited presenters. Sassen detailed the "creativity" of the intricate supply-chain network that should not be confined to the frame of the "creative class" and the power of heterogeneity that creative power could bring to the city. Yet the plan for creativity focused on its possibility to elevate Seoul's status to that of a "world-class city," especially through the new construction of Dongdaemun Design Plaza (DDP) (figure 5.3).

The ostentatious construction project DDP, at the end of the Cheonggyecheon stream's walk trail, embodied the desired "new flow" in its design and the "global" in its symbolic fame. Literally using a graphic tool to create an image of water, Zara Hadid, a world-renowned Iraqi-British architect, made a streamlined

FIGURE 5.3.   Dongdaemun Design Plaza around 9 p.m.

Photo by Euirock Lee.

and fluid-shaped building. The title for Hadid's competition-winning entry, *Metonymic Landscape,* suggests a foundational postmodern value: the space and people are "integrated and harmoniously mirroring each another."[9] Surrounded by box-shaped buildings with an inner grid layout to pack in as many store units as possible and in the quintessential Korean modern architecture style of commercial buildings and condominiums, the curved silver surface of DDP visually and intuitively suggested "newness." The DDP was exemplary of a trend among cities across Asia, where globally acclaimed architectural designers have been invited to work on the construction of public facilities, such as stadiums, airports, museums, or other monumental buildings, to create a charismatic spectacle in the city (Roy and Ong 2011). While previous cases of this kind of landmark construction served symbolic roles for the country's nation building and global attention, recent cases suggest a further aspiration to swiftly gentrify and redevelop former industrial cities (Ren 2008). Likewise, despite the very vague notion of "design" at the beginning of the planning phase, this new monument drove the most efficient transformation of the landscape and new sources of investment from multinational hotels and large conglomerates.

However, the whole construction process unfolded extremely rapidly and reproduced the tenacious bulldozing style of a constructivist move. And it was also partly due to the political interest in making this monument as a pinnacle of Oh's term of office. In 2008, the then-mayor Oh executed the demolition of Dongda-emun Stadium, a well-known landmark of the area since 1925, for the construction of DDP. Just as the Cheonggye overpass was demolished in a swift manner, the eighty-year-old stadium's deconstruction was fast-tracked. Not respected were the critical voices of those who cared for the historical value of the stadium, as a significant monument to the colonial period (1910–1945) and cultural legacy of the popularity of modern sports that emerged in the 1960s–1980s. Even the un-expected excavation of archeological remains from the Joseon period on the site—of city walls, wells, and a military facility—did not significantly interfere with the progress of the project. Some were prepared for public display, while others were removed and relocated to a different site.[10] In numerous interviews and the planning document, Hadid mentioned that she was inspired by and in-tended to express "the flow of Dongdaemun," the constant presence of people and commodities on the move,[11] many local critics viewed this flow as ultimately displaced from the actual movements of the people and the fabric of this space. It has been a widely known criticism that the short-term construction period did not include a stage in which the designer visited the site and might make an in-depth consideration of the social relations of the area.

A special issue of *Urban Drawings*, entitled, "The Hidden History of Dongda-emun Design Park and the Star Architect," chronicles the development history of DDP from its construction to the present. The articles and featured interviews by architects, activists, and artists commonly suggest that it is more important to consider the particular context of South Korean urban governance, where quick adjustment and execution have been promoted and tolerated for too long, than to blame the designer or dismiss the building itself. *Dongdaemun Design and His-tory Park Being Demolished in 2040*, a digital art piece by Listen to the City reprinted on the last page of the special issue, portrays an imagined future. In 2040, the DDP *will have decayed*, destined to be demolished and replaced, as the power shovel will have already begun digging up the ground and the crane made ready and on standby.[12] The artist asks, "How will we react when this celebrated and contested building becomes old?"[13] The image critically posits that the new build-ing, now a relic of the past, will likely be demolished again for the sake of pro-gress. The demolition of parts of the city has been so fast that it symbolically divides the past from the present, while its repeated reconstruction linearly pro-pels the city toward the future in great leaps and bounds. The original stadium stood eighty years on this site before it was demolished in service to modernity, the artwork suggests; in another thirty years, the demolition of the DDP will again be necessary to attain a more perfect future.

In a city where "the new" has held absolute power, markers of its industrial past are subject to the quick removal and easy replacement. New surface values of natural, global, and creative city have been a subject of heated debates and confrontations. Yet what it means to have a slow pace in the city is overshadowed by the possibility and the capacity of renewal. This developmentalist preoccupation with the new demarcates the past and the future in disjunctive stages of linear history and posits the present as a bounded stage between the past and the future. However, the aforementioned digital art by Listen to the City aptly reminds us that the present moment is situated along a continuum. Given that the new building has given rise to so much contestation, after decades, would we be happy to get rid of it, or should we care about its being throughout the decades, inscribed and imbued with people's trajectories, memories, and affects?

Commemorating the Past

If the Cheonggyecheon restoration and DDP construction projects redefined the present as a capacity for renewal by erasing the recent past to create a future, in the middle of the stream, another set of spatial practices have redefined the present as a capacity to commemorate the past. The monuments around the Chun Taeil bridge, including his statue and the tributary plaques, visibly show the contestations of the labor struggle, memorialize the past history, and imagine a better future.

In 2010, social organizations in Korea commemorated the fortieth anniversary of Taeil Chun's death. The Chun Taeil Foundation was already working with the city of Seoul since the completion of its restoration project in 2005 and successfully built a statue of Chun and tributary plaques on the bridge. The foundation furthered this effort to inscribe the history of labor activism around Cheonggyecheon stream and conducted a picketing campaign to have the bridge renamed Chun Taeil Bridge. During 2010, many individuals participated in this campaign, and the city of Seoul agreed to rename the bridge. The year was full of notable memorials for Korea's modern history besides the fortieth anniversary of Taeil Chun: the one hundredth anniversary of the Korea-Japan Annexation Treaty, the fiftieth anniversary of the Korean War, the fiftieth anniversary of the April Revolution, and the thirtieth anniversary of Gwangju Democracy Movement.[14]

The relatively "recent past" has not had a significant place in the master plan of Cheonggyecheon, as the Chun Taeil Bridge was the first and only bridge in the area to be named after a contemporary person. The names of the other bridges mostly reflect the history of the Joseon dynasty,[15] after artifacts were excavated during the demolition and uncovering process of Cheonggye stream and historic records. The celebration of "restoring" the distant past and the imagined original nature endorses the capacity of the current actor to execute the restoration in the present and to link the "betterment" with the city's future. The rise and decay

of the industrial city, represented by the daily presence of garment and other manufacturing sites in the area, symbolized the "dark face of modernization" that
needed to be overcome and left behind.[16]

Given this, the presence of the Chun Taeil Bridge has become a space that con-
jures up the recent past, making memories of social activism visible and tangible
in this landscape. While MANI has endeavored to have a similar impact on the
current garment and fashion industry by reinstating labor advocacy, those activists who invested in the Chun Taeil Bridge and his statue intervened in the physical landscape. The Chun Taeil Foundation intended the site to be a memorial
and an educational venue where people could learn about the recent history of
contestation and struggles of "ordinary people" (*minjung*).[17] Since then, the site
has become a destination for schools groups, religious groups, or activist
groups,[18] as well as a symbolic site where people support labor rights by paying
silent tribute or by leaving flower. Visiting this statue has become a symbolic
gesture for political leaders to show their support of the labor struggles in the
state-led manufacturing industry.[19] This physical and spatial construction of the
commemorative site echoes the rise of civil society in South Korea in the 2000s
and the proliferation of public monuments and archiving projects. In a similar
vein, state elites and planning projects have also gestured to leaving the emphasis
on rapid economic growth behind.[20] As such, urban monuments are not stable
objects: rather, they are open texts. The collective reflection on the political contestations opened a debate that produced disparate interpretations and desires
about the city's past, present, and future. Chun's statue evokes and is inscribed
with these various interpretations, imbuing the space with meanings about the
past and giving material form to people's desires for the future.

A Moment in the Present

While urban planners and campaign leaders intended Chun's statue to mark and
remember the past, the temporality of commemoration was unsettling for my
interlocutors. As Audra Simpson (2015) notes, commemoration assumes an
"eventful-ness" of the past and frames the present as "a time of reconciliation."[21]
Such reconciliation is a challenging task even for those who share the same perspectives on the past, as the present always reveals different pathways from the
moment to remember, which shapes the context of the moment of remember-
ing in different ways.

The way Oksun talked about the past involved ongoing pathways both in her
life and in the space. Our interviews mostly took place in Changshin-dong, where
MANI is located and to where she was commuting two days every week on the

subway. I asked her about what she thought about during her daily commute through the neighborhood, expecting to hear how it had looked when she had lived there or how she compared the current neighborhood with other parts of Seoul. Instead, Oksun answered: "I'm embarrassed [*changpihajyo*]. I drop my head and just walk fast [passing by the neighborhood], and I feel a pain in my chest. Sometimes I even take a different route [from where most factories are located]. Sometimes I tell myself to keep quiet about the labor activism because my whole life would have not meant anything."

Oksun's feelings were primarily focused on the working conditions of garment laborers, which have not been radically ameliorated since her own days. More importantly, Oksun was not seeing this condition from outside of it but while still working in the garment factories and interacting with people currently and actively working under those conditions. As I got to know two of her colleagues and good friends, Eunju and Sumi, I learned how their life diverged from and engaged with the past period being collectively remembered and recorded.

The three friends' stories show how life, labor, and activism are not separate experiences for many garment workers and are intimately tied with their own trajectories in the city itself. Oksun had been born and raised in the neighborhood and has never stopped working as a seamstress ever since she started work at age fourteen. Eunju, a fifty-seven-year-old former seamstress, was from a similar background, while Sumi, of a similar age, was from a rural town in Chungcheong Province. For poor or rural girls whose education was not fully supported by their families, "leaving for the city" or "commuting to somewhere every day on a regular basis" have constituted the ultimate modern, urban life, even though the work itself was arduous.

The three women started to work as seamstresses as teenagers and became involved in labor activism through night classes, where they were earning their general equivalency diploma. Back then, college and graduate students who were inspired by Chun's death were teaching the night classes for young factory workers, where they also imbued their students with an ideology of labor consciousness and solidarity. The desires to learn and to make social change were enmeshed for these teenagers, as well as their excitement to interact with young adults from different backgrounds. While having devoted their late teens, twenties, and thirties to labor activism, Oksun stayed on working as a full-time seamstress, and her two friends came in and out of factory work.

The period between the dismissal of the Cheonggye Garment Labor Union in 1981 by then-president Jeon Du-hwan's regime and the 1987 June Uprising marked the most dynamic time for protests among manufacturing laborers, students, activists, and garment workers in Dongdaemun, including the three friends, who helped organize the protests, support the activism, and, of course, care for their families. The aftermath of this period was more complex. My interlocutors talked about rough times that lingered for years, during which they felt that many parts of their lives fell apart. Sumi lost contact with her *oya*, a master seamstress with whom she had a strong partnership, which made her discouraged to be connected with the stitching work. After spending years working part-time jobs and volunteering for underprivileged children, Sumi had just made a decision to leave Seoul, where she had not been able to get away from an impoverished life with overwhelming debt, known as *hauseu pueo* (house poor). Eunju still works with other former union members for garment labor but found the rigor of the labor movement is not sustainable in the current situation. Oksun continued to work as seamstress, observing that students and activists gradually moved onto new sites of labor solidarity over the years. The shared idea was that they are constantly reminded that their past is still entangled with the ongoing marginalization of garment labor.

The three colleagues meet more frequently these days to talk about their past, as they attended commemorative events together in Cheonggyecheon. The three women all contributed money to the statue and the commemorative panel, and the name of their collective group is inscribed in a panel on the bridge. The historian Namhee Lee (2005) asserts that the hasty celebration of intellectuals' historical role in the labor movement of the 1980s has fed a feeling of nostalgia for a bygone era in the popular media. Moreover, it also carried a gendered implication for working women activists. For instance, Hyun Mee Kim (2001) argues that, working women's contributions to the 1987 labor movement and what happened afterward have been almost invisible in the popular discourse. They are mostly treated as "victims," if anything, compared to the well-publicized image of male workers and activists. Unlike intellectual activists, Oksun and her friends continued to live and work within the very setting that activists, media, and the state sought to foreclose as an historical site associated with a terminal moment in time (and therefore closed to the present). Oksun noted, "I wonder why it is so easy for them [other activists] to *look back* and talk about it. . . . That kind of luxury was never given to us." The absence of "luxury," which could also include gender or class differences, is articulated as a temporal position, on which one is not capable of putting a closure on the past to demarcate a different present. For Oksun and her friends, nostalgia for a time gone by is impossible since they continue to live and work within this space. The women's ongoing presence in Dongdaemun disrupts the dominant narrative of manufacturing and labor activism as being firmly rooted in the past. At the same time, continuing to work in the market also creates complex and conflicting feelings for Oksun, who must confront popular efforts to leave the past behind on her daily commute to the very garment factories that many people believe are obsolete.

Recently, a university professor approached Oksun and her colleagues to take part in a writing group for female laborers to record their life histories. The group was designed to help the women write autobiographical essays focusing on when they were actively involved in manufacturing work and union activities. The scholarly project shared the emerging idea that the union's official history did not record the subjective feelings of different generations and that it "flattened" the perspective of women like Oksun and her colleagues. The investigator explained to them that there was value in the collective writing process to record shared memories and to provide "cultural activities" for the participants who were reaching their fifties and sixties. However, the three women were hesitant to join the group since previous experiences providing testimony had not gone well. Eunju recalled:

> Like others, I have had interviews with scholars and the media. At that time, we lived a very precarious life, working in harsh conditions, being arrested for the first time in life, and still not seeing much change. Many of us either returned to work or drifted [to elsewhere] afterward. I have talked enough about what I did and what has happened, but I have not dealt with what I felt. . . . Now I see that I have a sort of disability [jangae] in my life when it comes to expressing myself. We were too young when we had such complex languages defining us [as labor], but we did not learn how to talk about what we did and what we felt.

Oksun told me that she had tried organizing her memories and writing them down several times but could not write more than a few sentences, so she decided to stop going to the writing group for a while. Oksun said she was hesitant because she was afraid of writing and felt blocked when trying to recall her past. While phrased in different ways, for the three women, the "block" or "disability" they felt when recounting their narratives suggests an inability in the current moment to coherently disarticulate their present lives from the period that is objectified in the statue's material form in the space. The activism had given them a frame to awaken their consciousness about labor exploitation and make sense of their political-economic position; however, it did not give them a way to think about their continued work in the factories or life after the union struggles. Oksun and her friends have not had closure on their experiences either through the commemoration of their activism or in mourning the partial successes and failures of the movement.

One day when I met with Oksun and Sumi together, they asked me if I had seen Chun's statue and what I thought about it. I told them truthfully that I found it meaningful to have the statue in the given location but that I was a bit perturbed that Chun is represented as just a torso. Sumi acknowledged my feeling and replied, "He looks very poor and sad, and he is too exposed to people just passing by." Oksun later added, "I like to see him there, but I don't like how pitiful he looks." As young night school students, the two women had been brought to that very spot to witness the burn marks on the ground where Chun had set himself on fire. The statue was not as impactful as the burn marks, they said. Sumi pointed out, "People just pass by, and they are mostly busy Dongdaemun people. Those who are enjoying the stream walk underneath the bridges and along the water and just pass by [Chun's statue], too. I think that is what will happen from now on. He doesn't look very glorious standing there." Although the radical transformation of Cheonggyecheon stream and the unveiling of Chun's statue were initially inspiring, they are now the unremarkable backdrop to people's everyday lives. The history, like the water, flows away.

Grappling with their own personal histories, Oksun and her friends found it easier to discuss their feelings about Chun's struggle. The women's empathy for Chun's statue focused on an affective connection to the object's persistent presence in the present. The statue, firmly fixed on the street beside the Cheonggyecheon stream, surrounded by quick-service motorbikes and fast-moving passersby, attempts to place a particular moment of life and work in the past. However, what does it mean to be "figures of the past" through which the past is remembered and recounted, while one is actively working in the same profession? For Oksun and her friends, their complex feelings about the unresolved past are entangled with their unarticulated present and an uncertain future.

Chun's commemoration project renders a material, symbolic, and social break in a linear narrative in which history marches forward, carried along in the spectacle of the Cheonggyecheon stream revitalization project. Techniques of liberal urban governance strive to erase certain histories, while bridging the distant (valued) past with the material landscape of the present and a desired future. However, the monument succeeded in shifting the politics of memory by drawing public attention to the Cheonggyecheon labor movement. Simultaneously, my interlocutors' reluctance to narrate their own past or to commemorate the events of their lives as truly complete reveals a disjunction in the way differently positioned actors recount, desire, and experience time in this place. Oksun and her friends have not experienced a clear break between the past and the present and so find themselves "out of place" in a narrative that sets their life events in a time apart. For these women, conflicting accounts of the past and the present, and even differing desires for the future, comingle to produce an unsettling feeling of temporal dislocation. Oksun and her friends' discomfort with dominant celebratory narratives of a past they continue to experience highlights the way that urban built environments are uneven, contested terrains through which people express conflicting memories, feelings, and desires.

Conclusion: Disturbing Vitality in the Deadly Flow

In August 2010, the same year of the fortieth anniversary of Chun's death and the renaming of Chun Taeil Bridge, there was an incident spurred by the unexpected discovery of a small fish called sweetfish, *euneo*, in the Cheonggyecheon stream. It is a species of fish that usually thrives in fresh, abundant river water. Authorities argued that the presence of the sweetfish was visible, living proof of the stream's successful restoration and the ecosystem that enjoys 468 kinds of flora and fauna living in or alongside the Cheonggyecheon stream.[22] However, the news was immediately followed by cynical comments and posts that went viral on online bulletin boards and social networks, by those who doubt the origin and authenticity of the fish.

Indeed, it was hard to believe that the fish could possibly be a "natural" one. The fish is often found in the Seomjin River and other rivers in the southwest part of South Korea. Would it swim all the way from there? There was a theory that it was one of a big batch that the government had released in the Han River the past year, as part of the campaign to promote the biodiversity in the Han River. Still, if it swam against stream to somehow arrive in Cheonggyecheon, its survival was even more unthinkable news. The primary problem is the uniform and rapid speed of the water's flow in straight line. While serving as a nice image of the stream's lively flow and for self-purification, the stream's flow would not slow down for living nutrients to take hold and serve a proper habitat for small creatures like a sweetfish.

A few months after I returned from an extensive period of fieldwork, the sweetfish was reported. At first, I found this incident resonating with many comments about the stream that I had heard from my interlocutors in passing. Of course, it was not the first or only species that was discovered and then disputed in the stream; horn shells, dark chub, and other living species that live in the shallow part of stream had been found occasionally and then contested, before and after the sweetfish.[23] Later I received updates with more of these rumors and doubts and wrote about how they serve as an outlet for public opinions toward the radical transformations of Seoul's landscape. The public cynicism was not just an environmentalist concern but doubt and fatigue toward the city's long-standing and persistent obsession with expedited urban planning and boastful celebration of it. Therefore, the sweetfish—as an authentic marker of the viability of the flow—simultaneously underscores the aspiration of "green development" and belies it.

Meanwhile, the timing of this news made it more than just fresh information about the "context" of my field site. In the moment, as I was desperately trying to find my own analytic standpoint, taking in the piles of interview scripts, field notes, articles, and books, the subsequent comments and posts made me think about the incident along with the narratives of my interlocutors and their presence. For those who are critical about urban planning, this sweetfish and its survival are disturbing. We now *know* that the fast and straight flow, the icon of the ugly past, makes this sweetfish's survival doubtful. What should we do with this life that somehow survived and lives in the present? While out of place, should this life, somehow existing in the present, be ignored or cared for? I had similar questions when I talked with Eunae, whose comment about passion was introduced earlier in chapter 3, and many others who talked about their affection for their work. We all know that in this fast-fashion manufacturing scene, passion, attachment, and affection are hard to retain. But for those who are talking about it, despite their awareness that it could sound "cheesy" (as Eunae described) or "unrealistic" and "unnatural" from the critical perspective, these attributes are not external to the histories of the marketplace, the factories, and the city, rendering a singular conclusion or a complete critique.

I find parallels in the ambiguous vitality of the sweetfish and in the ongoing presence of the three women in the market and their uneasiness toward Chun's commemorative statue. The memorial campaign made a critical break from the government's narrative of a soft, creative, and slow-paced global city full of the promise of the future. Rather, Chun's dark, heavy torso is a symbol of mass manufacturing and violent labor protests and impedes the open view of the Cheonggyecheon stream. The statue draws people in to learn about the past, to revive the past, or to reconcile with the past. Within this urban crowd of observers and visitors (who have differing relationships with the past they are seeing in the statue), my interlocutors' perspective is ambiguous. They move around the city, from the old neighborhood to the new landscape of Cheonggyecheon, their regular factories and MANI, and various meeting locations with their friends, activists, and intellectuals. Their complex feelings in these movements do not render a strong resistance to the new landscape but challenge a clear division between the past and present and a notion of a linear progression through which the present replaces the past. The history of labor in their lived experience was not fully contained in the discursive and physical representation in the space.

potential themes:

1: "Fast paced" 2: "Slow paced"

temporality?

3: History + Attachment 4: Passion + Affection

Labor

CONCLUSION

It was my third interview with Oksun when we talked about what she thought about her sewing skills, the conversation that opened this book in the prologue. By then we had talked about the trajectories of her job, her role and experience at MANI, and her thoughts about Dongdaemun and Cheonggyecheon. I had also gotten to meet with her friends Eunju and Sumi. As we talked, she moved the fabric on the sewing machine, and the jacket she was making began to take form. Her narrative conjured a picture for me of the changes in the market over the decades Oksun had worked there. Although I had spoken with her many times through informal and semiformal interviews, and my regular participation in MANI classes where she taught, this particular conversation stood out. It was the first time she talked directly about her own work at length, and it was a rare moment that my interlocutor talked about the speed of stitching beyond quantitative efficiency and exploitation.

Oksun highlighted the ways in which her long life of work and activism made it difficult for her to come to terms with her advanced sewing skills. It was due to the conflict she had to negotiate between the critiques of labor exploitation and the motivation she gained through her own work as a garment seamstress. When she was younger, Oksun's life was always busy and intense, as she worked both for the union and the factory. Her family's livelihood, as well as the union, relied heavily on her labor. Even after mass production and labor unionism dwindled in Dongdaemun, Oksun never stopped working, moving from one factory to another, and mastering stitching skills. However, Oksun told me that she refrained from indulging in her experienced skills because she had been taught that to do so would undermine her own awareness of the labor conditions. In the realm of labor consciousness and solidarity that she learned from the union activism, her individual achievement and motivation to be productive and efficient would only reproduce the brutal speed of material production and further her own exploitation.

Oksun has only recently begun to claim her skills as she has observed the commemorative projects and physical changes in and around the areas of Cheonggyecheon and Dongdaemun. Oksun was also inspired by her encounters with people who became newly involved in sewing and had returned to the marketplace via MANI. Projects like MANI revealed the complicated and conflicting sense of time in work, the market, and the city. More significantly for my interlocutors, projects like these, while entailing contradictory logics and results, create a small opening in the present through which Oksun was confronted with the ability that she had developed throughout her lifetime. The ambivalence with which she faced her skill, however, points to the complex and shifting meanings people attach to work, places, and time. In discussing her feelings about her skill, Oksun did not deny the backbreaking pressure of working for the speed of material production and circulation. Rather, for those like Oksun who live in the day-to-day speed of the market, attachment and passion offered a language through which to make sense of and to explain how they persist in this extreme working context.

The moment of "pure concentration," as she said in the interview quoted in the prologue, makes full sense only when we take this whole narrative into account. The moment when she found herself making a smooth line of stitch without consulting anybody or being directed and affirmed her devotion to accomplish it was not a happening on one given day or a general self-compliment. It was a consciously chosen moment that she decided to convey to a student researcher (who I was at the time) who asked when and how her feelings about work had changed. Her persistent and resilient work and her own attachment to it would not find a proper place in the critical perspective toward the marginalization of garment labor, the reflections of the linear history of the past labor movement and the new trend of market experiments, and the fast-forwarded urban renewal projects inscribing the past and future of the city. As explored in chapter 5, Oksun did not have the "privilege" of bearing witness to the past nor did she find it in the grand future along Cheonggyecheon. While being in the midst of these locations, in the accelerated urban marketplace, her narrative on the swift and apt stitching machine created a slim opening to the present. And this opening serves similarly to the way "passion" was a common word for Eunae and other workers who expressed an attachment to their work (chapter 3). As Lauren Berlant discusses, the state of attachment or enthusiasm gives a sense of one's place in the world (Berlant 2011). In the world that would not let these attachments manifest due to the historical and discursive predicaments, this opening amplified our optical focus to see the quick but fine moment of attunement of her laboring body, sewing machine, and the material commodity, and Oksun's historical consciousness and care about her own work.

Oksun's earlier dilemma toward her skill highlights the ethnographic challenge to analyze the problem of speed: inasmuch as our critique of labor is tied with the abstracting force of speed, it is also hard to translate people's experiences and feelings outside the frame of abstracting, alienating speed. Throughout the chapters, I have highlighted narrative moments that exist within, are produced by, and respond to the problem of speed. The stories I shared in this book demonstrate that the speed of modern times and the accelerated, unceasing productivity that goes along with it are not possible without human practices that relate with and build attachments to others, commodities, and work itself. These labor practices constitute the very dynamic of the fast speed of production but also inevitably create a flow of life that is dense and messy. This humanness even slows industrial coordination to people's own pace in conducting their everyday routines and family lives. A fast-paced, proximate engagement with clothes led my interlocutors to find and express their own passion, which resulted in spontaneous moments through which value was created. Short, fast cycles of garment making, while incredibly labor intensive, also enabled designers and seamstresses to develop a physical and emotional attachment to the clothes they made and to enjoy subtle moments of creativity. The work of women like Oksun, their interactions with each other, and the mobility of bodies at work all materially and affectively animated the nighttime space for both observers and the workers themselves. Individual, collective, and institutional practices and imaginations concerning the relationship between work and time illuminate the specific dynamics in which subjective experiences of pace, currents, and cycles constitute and sustain the complexity of speed in the 24-hour city of Seoul.

I often drew my walking trajectories or followed walk-throughs of my interlocutors to set up an inquiry for chapters thus far. The introduction started with a walk-through of Dongdaemun marketplace with a designer, and chapter 5 ended with tracing the narratives of the current and former seamstresses walking down to the Cheonggyecheon stream. With these figures, I was following the movement of people, commodities, and the atmosphere through time. The vantage point of a walk-through was not only my literal entry into the field but also served as a point of analysis in this ethnography. Immersed in the multiple rhythms, paces, and histories of Dongdaemun, I grounded my argument that the speed of material production and circulation heavily relies on the embodied labor of workers and their attachment to work, and it is more problematic to simplify the tempo-rality of work or to assume that one could stand outside the critique of it. To dif-ferent degrees of elaboration, garment workers and activists were imbued with the critiques of fast-fashion manufacturing, the growth-centrism of rapid indus-trialization, and its impact on the devaluation of their own labor. Despite or against the critical perspectives, they endeavored to sustain and understand the intensity of the work for extended times through the day and through their lives.

To sustain the fast-fashion marketplace and the 24-hour city, workers bring in and cultivate dense relationships among people, things, and space, in recalibrating their lives. This ethnography aimed to expand our understanding and analysis of the multifaceted temporality of work by paying attention to these practices. Of course, there have been explicit frames of analysis. Most factory workers, designers, and traders were working incessantly for the one-day or two-day spans of produc-tion orders. The wholesale and retail plaza's business hours are fixed at night, and the traders need to keep up with them. Yet these temporal structures are partial and cannot entirely explain the different senses of and everyday practices on time.

More nuanced analysis starts with attention to particular conditions. As Tsing (2009) notes, it is not so much a hierarchical system that centrally organizes the manufacturing process but rather a codependent and precarious set of relation-ships keeping the supply chain moving. In the intricate and intimate supply chain I traced from nighttime wholesaling, daytime designing, stitching, finishing, and wholesaling again, one's absence or lateness at work would directly affect other people's daily household income and their personal relationships. The rhythms and tempos of family duties, care, trust, and intimacy inherently en-meshed with the shortened cycle of production and circulation. The life course of the commodities is extremely short in this fast-fashion industry. In the case of Dongdaemun, the quick pace of life is only made possible through people's long-term experiences and sense of attachment to the skills they use to produce those commodities. The intensity and energy of these actors creating the commodities are not only carried by the final product but are also affectively transmitted to the space and others by occupying and moving with them across the space of the marketplace and the city. And this transmission of affect smoothly operates, ani-mates, and commodifies the 24-hourization of the city.

By emphasizing affect, intimacy, and passion, I challenge a quick and simplis-tic application of the alienating power of material speed, the well-known Marxist theory that posits that workers under capitalism are estranged from other labor-ers, the products of their labor, and the act of labor itself. In the first part of the book, I looked at the process through which these types of affect, intimacy, and passion reflect and further generate the dense and nuanced relationships of com-modity production and circulation, sustaining the factories and marketplace in the city. And the second part revealed how these underlying relations complicated the problematization of speed by social and state projects to control the speed of the marketplace and the city. The analytic focus on narratives and microscopic relations does not necessarily stand against a structural understanding of the precarity of labor but highlights the complexities of relationship between embodied labor and the city. First, the dense relationships between people, commodities, and labor construct the very conditions of just-in-time production and reveal the social and affective aspects of the physical proximity and temporal immediacy, the very nature of "flexibility" of the site. Second, the analyses reveal the various values that are produced within and outside the domains of wage labor. Third, the book reveals how the workers' practices connect the time and space of life and labor and are deeply connected in constructing the 24-hour city of Dongdaemun and broader Seoul. The city space is intersected and temporalized by these practices and, in turn, reminds people of the longer passage of time that went along with their lives.

The scale of analysis for theories of capitalism has been very macro focused. Analyses often attribute the problem of speed to flexible accumulation, the nature of the industrial and postindustrial city of modern and postmodern times, or cultures of information and communication technology. In contrast, this book explored the ways the pursuits of fast accumulation are not merely a theoretical problem but a social problem for local activists, workers, policy makers, and ethnographers connected through labor, moral, historical, and urban concerns. These place-based and locally specific layers of problems ultimately challenge the possibility of singular and universal politics of speed and their impact on everyday lives. MANI and city planners said the sped-up market and culture were wrong and decided to intervene to control its speed, but the artificial slowing down revealed the incongruent temporalities within them, complicating the politics of critique. As people become more aware of and respond to the problematization of their work through efforts like those of MANI and the state's projects, the presence and contradictions of these attachments become more apparent and complicate labor and urban politics.

The city's history unfolds in unpredictable path. After the extensive period of my fieldwork, during the years 2012–2018, the Changsin-dong area went through a new phase of "urban regeneration." Mayor Wonsoon Park implemented a community-centered urban planning project and declared, again, "a paradigm shift" from the top-down approach done by his predecessors Myungbak Lee, who led the Cheonggyecheon stream restoration, and Sehoon Oh, who led the Design Seoul project, as introduced in chapter 5. Changsin-dong was appointed as the first and most prominent case for this planning. Its longtime marginalization as a factory town for Dongdaemun market and the presence of small-scale factories inspired social activists, artists, and scholars to push for the local revitalization. The shabby alleys and streets became a resource to preserve, some of which were presented as a living "Museum of Sewing Factory Streets." In preparing a short writing on this change (see S. Park 2019b), I found the interviews and life story accounts of my formal interlocutors featured in media and archival works. The marginalization gained new relevance as a forefront of the planning project for a future change. The intricate network of garment manufacturing and their 24-hour operation became an object for public view and a photo spot for blogs and social networks.

On my latest visit to the factory area in 2019, while I was strolling around the neighborhood I ran into one of my interlocutors. He showed me an archive booklet of the neighborhood that he kept in his factory. Conducted after I was done with my main fieldwork, the archive project reflected the new attention given to the neighborhood and initiatives to document the local history for the urban regeneration program. He was happy to point out a photo in the book of a gathering of factory workers in the alley, which happened to include me in the corner. I was holding a camera in my hand taking a picture of the gathering, unaware that a photo was being taken of me. In my ethnographic work, I tried to analyze how the past, present, and future have been articulated through policies and practices, but my observations and presence no longer allowed me to stand outside of it. Just as I have never had a full view of the marketplace either. The view was partial in that it was at a particular point in time as well. Depending on whose tempo I was following, when I was talking to people, and where we were in the cycle of commodities and everyday life, the perspectives and relationships to life and labor take multiple shapes, with an opening and a closure in different times.

Acknowledgments

The process of writing this book has included multiple phases of acceleration, deep stagnation, incessant pauses, and repeated delays over many years. Every moment along the way, I have received tremendous help from people and institutions who guided me, pushed me forward, waited for me, and walked with me.

First, I would like to extend my appreciation to many individuals in Dongdaemun and Seoul, most of whom are presented in the book with pseudonyms to protect their anonymity. I am deeply grateful to the individual interlocutors I interacted with during the fieldwork. My presence and interviews interrupted their busy lives, yet they still accepted me into their space, allowed me tag along as they worked, and shared their life stories. The insights I learned from them not only formed this book but will continue to shape the way I live as a laborer and a woman. I also thank the organization I pseudonymously called MANI, who allowed me to participate in and observe their projects and shared their valuable insights into the garment labor movement.

I started this research at the University of California, Irvine, where I learned the excitement of working as an anthropologist. I had the great fortune to find mentorship from Bill Maurer, Mei Zhan, and Inderpal Grewal, whose passion for anthropological and feminist thinking have affected the way I read, write, and talk about the world. I am grateful to have had the opportunity to learn from and share my ideas with Julia Elyachar, Kavita Philip, Kaushik Sunder Rajan, and Jennifer Terry. For the brilliant and inspirational learning community, I thank Nanao Akanuma, Christina Bajarano, Allison Fish, Nalika Gajaweera, Erin Huang, Yunjong Lee, Alexandra Lippmann, Caroline Melly, Natalie Newton, Hyeonseon Park, and Lien Vu. My life has also been greatly supported by the friendship and guidance of Kiza and Jennifer Suh.

The rudimentary idea of this research was formed at Yonsei University. The professors and students at Yonsei provided me with a firm foundation for my personal and intellectual development. Hyun Mee Kim has been the ultimate source of inspiration, advice, and mentorship for nearly two decades. I appreciate Yoonkeyong Nah and Chohan Haejoang for their teaching and mentoring, both of which have been influential in the way I practice research and teaching. I am grateful for the thoughtful comments and friendship of Jeongmin Kim, Jiyoon Kim, Jonghwa Kwon, and Suebinn Lee. I also thank those who were in the Ethnography

Methods seminar and the Space reading group in 2009 for their feedback and collegiality for my in-progress fieldwork.

Alternative Culture (Ttohanaeui Munhwa), a prominent feminist organization in South Korea, turned my personal interest in Dongdaemun into a scholarly one. Working for the organization's short project Seoul as Women's Space, in 2005, I developed my perspective on nighttime Dongdaemun, seeing it as constructed by various women's material and affective labor, their attachment to clothes, and their economic aspirations. I also thank Haksil Kim for her intellectual contribution to the project and longtime friendship.

A postdoctoral fellowship at the Korea Studies Institute at the University of Southern California allowed me to be part of the vibrant Korean studies community in Southern California. David Kang has been always welcoming and giving concerning professional advice. Yeongmin Choe, Sandra Fahy, Sunyoung Park, and the students and fellow scholars that I met through numerous workshops and events at USC provided constructive feedback.

At Scripps College and the Claremont Colleges, I have had the luxury of working with colleagues who have given me consistent inspiration, support, and intellectual insights. Lara Deeb has given me tremendous guidance since the day we first met, the kind of guidance that a junior colleague can only dream of. I am also lucky to have another fantastic colleague in Gabriela Morales, whose intellectual rigor and insights have enriched my work at Scripps. I am grateful to the exciting anthropology community, including Emily Chao, Marianne De Laet, Dru Gladney, Joanne Nucho, Dan Segal, and Claudia Strauss. I would not have made it through the exciting and challenging years as a junior faculty without the friendship of Pey-yi Chu and Ghenwa Hayek. Piya Chaterjee, Jih-Fei Cheng, Angelina Chin, Kim Drake, Julie Liss, Albert Park, and Carmen San Juan generously provided their warmth and wisdom, which helped me grow as a member of the community and develop this research further.

Scholars in the field of cultural anthropology, urban studies, and Korea studies have offered invaluable conversations and feedback on earlier drafts of this book. Two SSRC Korean Studies Workshops were major venues that came in handy during writing phases. I thank Jun Yoo for his ceaseless support of junior scholars. I was lucky to have feedback from Nicole Constable, Seungsook Moon, and fellow participants. I appreciate the scholars and readers whose sharp and rigorous feedback have helped me develop this book: Mun Young Cho, Hae Yeon Choo, Jennifer Chun, Sujin Eom, Laam Hae, Juhui Judy Han, Jungwon Kim, Hyeseon Jeong, Hong Kal, Jiyeon Kang, Eunjeong Kim, Eunshil Kim, June Hee Kwon, Pardis Mahdavi, Sinwoo Lee, S. Heijin Lee, John Lie, Hirokazu Miyazaki, Christina Moon, Laura Nelson, YouJeong Oh, Bae-Gyoon Park, Doyoung Song, and Thuy Tu. Rachael Joo has given me personal and scholarly support through our long-term friendship. Eleana Kim served as a discussant and offered in-depth feedback at the manuscript workshop at Scripps. I thank Jesook Song for her generous mentorship across multiple occasions and locations. I am grateful that I was able to have mentorship from and share memories of Nancy Abelmann, who always encouraged my work from fieldwork to publications.

Various stages of research and writing for this book were supported by a Wenner Gren Foundation Fieldwork Grant; merit-based scholarship at the School of Social Sciences and short-term research grants from the Department of Anthropology, the School of Social Sciences, the Center for Asian Studies, and the Center for Global Peace and Cooperation at UC Irvine; Faculty Research Funds from Fredrick Chau; and Faculty Research Funds and Sabbatical Research Funds from Scripps College. The Scripps Anthropology Department sponsored a manuscript workshop. The research was also supported by EnviroLab Asia and Henry Luce Foundation.

Part of the book was originally published as "Stitching the Fabric of Family: Time, Work, and Intimacy in Seoul's Tongdaemun Market" in the *Journal of Korean Studies* 17, no. 2: 383–406, © 2012, The Trustees of Columbia University in the City of New York. All rights reserved. Republished by permission of the copyright holder and the present publisher, Duke University Press (www.dukeupress .edu). I appreciate the anonymous reviewers and editors who helped enhance the analyses and allowed me to include their content in this book.

I am grateful to the editors, reviewers, and professionals who helped me bring this project to fruition. Anita Grisales and Philip Watrous helped edit earlier drafts. At Cornell, I deeply appreciate Jim Lance, the acquisitions editor, for his patience and encouragement throughout the whole process. I extend gratitude to Clare Jones, Mary Gendron (at Westchester Publishing Services), Mary Kate Murphy, and Brock Schnoke. The very last phase of the book's production happened during the COVID-19 pandemic and wildfire crises in California, and they have shown incredible professionalism and sympathy. Two anonymous reviewers' invaluable feedback made a critical impact on the revision of the book, the kind of feedback that I will continue to engage with throughout my scholarship. Bart Wright offered prompt work and endless patience in making numerous revisions to the maps. I was honored to work with Euirok Lee, who produced several photos that appear in the book.

Jieun Lee, Erin Moran, and Erica Vogel have been the most precious collaborators in my journey for this project. There is no corner in this book that does not carry multiple layers of their intellectual engagement and friendship.

Finally, I thank my family for their untiring support and affectionate critique of my work and my life.

Notes

PROLOGUE

1. To protect my research participants' anonymity, throughout this book I have omitted or merged some identifying details of their lives and used pseudonyms. Names of small-scale businesses such as independent shops and factories have also been altered. All translations of Korean and English are mine unless otherwise specified.

2. I am using a pseudonym for MANI.

3. This book follows the Revised Romanization of Korean system of transliteration, except for widely used names of places and people, including Chun Taeil, Park Chung-hee, and Lee Myung-bak.

4. A part of this interview quote also appeared in my other work (Park 2019a).

INTRODUCTION

1. This Koreanized English word was the name of a delivery company and has become a general term for delivery services via motorbike or light commercial vehicle.

2. While Michael Piore and Charles Sable (1984)'s term "flexibility" address the widespread transition in the mode of production on a global scale, the authors also emphasize a system embedded in the local sociocultural context and close spatial ties.

3. Even in the early period, the marketplace tended to be specialized in the fabric and garment trade.

4. Pyeonghwa sijang (Pyeonghwa marketplace) or Donghwa sijang (Donghwa marketplace) are the names of multistory wholesale plazas, where individual merchant-run independent shops design, produce, and sell their own goods. These shop owners, that is, tenants in each building, also organize themselves as merchants' associations for each "marketplace" (Kim, Lee, and Ahn 2004, 143–45).

5. For the process of labor mobilization in the garment industry and class struggles of this period, see S.-K. Kim (1997); Koo (2000).

6. The harsh working conditions in Cheonggyecheon, the street where the most prominent factories in the Dongdaemun area were located, spurred vehement activism in the form of garment labor unions, which formed the front line of democratic movements against the military government. Consequently, union activism in Dongdaemun holds a significant place in South Korean contemporary activist history surrounding labor rights, political liberty, and social equality and justice (S. K. Cho 1985; J. Choi 1989; S. Chun 2003; Lee and Song 1994).

7. David Harvey (1989) delineated the model of a "shrunk globe" in which images and commodities cascade into the metropolitan center. His primary interest reveals that space and time are socially constructed through the mode of production, the technological development of transportation, and communication. From this, Harvey framed our experiences of time as a "sense of acceleration" determined by the fast turnover of commodities and capital.

8. The factories and wholesalers within the Dongdaemun area are connected with Korean and foreign retailers and wholesalers via contracted merchandising agencies called *peuromosyeon* (promotion) agencies in Korea, working with small-scale apparel compa-

nies or single-person, online businesses in Korea and other "close" countries, such as Japan and China.

9. For instance, Lehman Brothers invested approximately $60,000,000 in one of the newly launched shopping malls in Seoul, which led to its utter failure due to the company's bankruptcy in 2008 when major investment banks collapsed amid the liquidity crisis.

10. Gender and race ideologies have devalued the labor of certain groups as "unskilled" and justified the devaluation of such labor (Collins 2002; Fraser 1989; Green 1996). The strong contrast between the "unskilled and simplistic repetition" of stitching and the "complex, skilled work" of pattern making or fabric cutting is very much gendered in that the former is commonly associated with women's naturalized traits and the latter with traits thought innate to men. When something is considered women's work, the knowledge, practice, aptitude, or abilities required to complete it are typically seen as belonging to a lower skill level. It is precisely through this logic that the export-centered garment manufacturing industry mobilized a major sector of young, working-class, underprivileged women and justified the undervaluing of their labor from the 1960s to the 1980s (S.-K. Kim 1997). More specifically, in the Korean case, these women were also placed subservient to the state and the family due to a paternalistic, Confucian cultural ideology (H. M. Kim 2001).

11. During this time, workers began organizing alongside intellectuals and students to raise awareness of and improve their conditions. But as garment manufacturing companies chased lower labor costs to Ho Chi Minh City, Bangladesh, or Guangzhou, union activism in Dongdaemun also started to diminish due to labor-market flexibility, privatization, and neoliberal economic restructuring (J. Chun 2011).

12. As Suzanne Bergeron (2004) argues, women often become a target for the control and construction of the national economy in economic development policy.

13. In this sense, women laborers were constantly conceived as Other in the desire for modernity during the South Korean industrialization and modernization period of the 1960s–1980s and again in 1990s–2000s, because of the desire to relegate images of "rapid industrialization" to the past. Garment labor has persistently been subject to the gendered ideology of modernity as a theoretical and discursive construct in East Asia (Rofel 1999).

14. For example, Jonathan Crary (2013); Robert Hassan (2007). For the implication of global cities, see Richard G. Smith (2003). Sarah Sharma (2014, 5–7) also offers a thorough and theoretical review on this topic.

15. Wajcman (2014, 172) suggests that we see how speed could be experienced as multiple ways and speed could be productive of complex social disparities by focusing on human interactions with information technologies, transformation, and time-saving domestic technologies. Based on a similar methodological interest, Sharma (2014, 6–7) suggests seeing people's everyday experiences and their differentiated relations to disciplinary power in time. For other nuanced understandings of modern time in its multiple chronotopes and temporalities, see Bear (2014); Miyazaki (2003).

16. A series of feminist works has criticized the use of "modern" as a totalizing, epoch-making concept that has been overused by Korean leftist intellectuals (H. M. Kim 2001). For example, Haejoang Cho (1998) qualifies her usage of "compression" and "acceleration" as based on her critical stance toward the very modern and masculine notion of historical processes that does not allow different representation of histories. "Compression" for Cho is not something that erodes the specificities of local life but prevents them from unfolding, which would later belie the inability of the pure notion of growth and development. Nancy Abelmann (2003) uses "compression" to refer to a notion of rapid modernity that ethnographers and their informants share but with different meanings and usages attached to education, social mobility, masculinity, and family.

17. MANI's social enterprise also includes contestations over free market ideas. I draw on the anthropologist Julia Elyachar's (2005) discussion of NGO and civil organizations

that further the market economy with different techniques for the creation and distributions of value.

1. AFFECTIVE CROWDS AND MAKING THE 24-HOUR CITY

1. Scholarly and popular literatures have documented the "cultural planning" of nighttime spaces. In many locations around the globe, especially in the former industrial centers of Europe and the United States, state planning and corporate actors have brought about coherent urban revitalization by creating a cultural economy and drawing the creative classes (Bianchini 1995; Chatterton and Hollands 2003; Hadfield 2015; Hae 2012).

2. See chapter 2 for a detailed explanation of the term *home-factory*.

3. My analysis aligns with the work of Hatfield (2010, 23–26), who conceptualized the Taiwanese valuation of the urban atmosphere, "heat and noise," as a temporal term, "crowd time." The bustling noise, light, and heat of crowds generate collectivities of being together, making the time of the city visible and forming sensuous qualities of place.

4. The term *Homo nightcus* is designated as an "imported" word in the *Open Dictionary*, a user-based dictionary run by the National Research Council of Korea that includes various colloquial words of the time (https://opendict.korean.go.kr/dictionary/view?sense_no=1373696). The term is a sort of Korean wordplay using English and Latin to make it "sound like" a scholarly denomination of a human subspecies.

5. Terms such as *-sede* (generation) or *-jok* (type) are not rare in contemporary urban Korea, where people talk about certain practices of the young generations. Among these names, *homo* seems to be indicative of the type of people adopting and changing the social ecology of everyday life. So, in phrases that use *homo* plus a Latin-sounding word, they are playing with the idea of a different species of human. A similar wordplay composition applies to *Homo TVcus* or *Homo digicus* (J. Yoon 2009).

6. The mode of liberation loosened other modes of social control: for example, new policies lifted the mention of school uniforms, called off restrictions on travel abroad, and allowed men to have long hair. The liberal economy benefited from this "liberation of nighttime," as 24-hour factories brought about rapid industrialization.

7. For an extensive review of the campaign in the year 2000, see Eun Young Heo's (2000) work on the reduction of labor hours in South Korea.

8. Haejaong Cho (2015, 446) described this hype as a feature of "spec generation," contemporary Korean youth who are under the pressure of cultivating qualifications that are translatable in a career market.

9. I borrow the notion of containment from Teressa Brennen's (2004) *Transmission of Affect*, in which she has theorized the dissemination and spread of affect, passion, emotion, and desire and challenged the strong assumption of energetically and emotionally self-contained individuals in accounting for their behavior. Macdalena Pettersson McIntyre (2014) also observed how this kind of affect and passion in fashion workers are transferred to others and ultimately commodified. I agree with McIntyre's description of this process, in that it needs to be distinguished from structured management, as it is inherently ongoing, unpredictable, and nonreductive (92).

10. Kim (2008) published a book on this experience and has come to represent the new commerce of Dongdaemun online. . In her book, Kim explained how she used to watch people's fashion, the loops buyers make in the building or the cycles of items in Dongdaemun. Kim described the experience like "walking in a forest" full of clothes and people. Her story speaks to many others I met who were running retail boutiques and shops in other areas of Seoul, in Dongdaemun mall, and online.

11. A media report suggested that, while other items were increasing, the fashion apparel sector still took up 40 percent of online shopping malls in 2011 and stayed as the most chosen start-up item for years (H. Yoon 2013).

12. *Sunbogeum Gyohoe Sinmun* [Full Gospel Church news], September 2, 2012, 6.

13. *Sunbokeum Gyohoe Sinmun*, April 28, 2012, 9.

14. The first predawn prayer meetings were recorded in Pyeongyang in 1906 (Lamport 2018, 431). In 2000, some mega churches such as Myeongseon held intense predawn prayer meeting sessions in March and September that were congregated by more than 50,000 attendants a day, for multiple days. These meetings have contributed to its exponential growth since 1980, from a small office in a corner of a commercial building to a megachurch with 100,000 members. In addition, other churches held special sessions—often more frequently than once a month or on a more regular basis. Special prayer meetings in South Korean churches have become a major driving force for their growth.

15. A *Hangyeorye* newspaper article introduced scholarly and religious attention to the predawn prayers as uniquely Korean, and as a "localized form of global religion of Christianity that immersed in Korean's spiritual culture." Hwadong Seo, "Myeongseong gyohoe sebyeok gido, maeil 7manmyeongssik moyeo" [70,000 people attended the daily predawn prayers of Myeongseong Church], *Hangook gyeongje*, March 7, 2012.

16. The critiques point out that some dawn prayers take the form of massive revivals and that the size of those events are used as a numeric measurement of devotion. Drawing such attention to growth-centered developmentalism and the heated competition among megachurches has been a major aspect of the criticism directed at Korean evangelical Christianity. Dawn prayer meetings have rapidly mobilized large populations and have played a significant role in the expansion and growth of Korean churches. Critical voices are also concerned with escalating tendencies: the strict obsession of the formality of time rather than the quality and concentration of the prayers or the pressure on attendance rather than voluntary participation (e.g., Rhee, undated).

17. For example, Chanho Park and Jaecheon Gu's (2010) edited volume *Saebyeok Gidohaneun CEO* offers success stories by famous CEOs; Aron Park (2011) has introduced the well-known cases of three churches and suggests predawn prayer is a "cultural commodity for exportation" (*munhwa suchul sangpum*).

18. Time management, according to Seo's analysis of the proliferating self-help manuals and self-development essays of neoliberal South Korea, is at the center of the emerging field of "successology" (*seongkonghak*), whether it emphasizes the ethos of dawn, number of hours, productive time, or fun time. Ultimately, time management is based on techniques that are already entrepreneurial.

2. INTIMATE NETWORKS

1. See the discussions regarding genealogies of "social time" by Susan Hanson and Geraldine Pratt (1995); Nancy Folbre (2004); and Carmen Leccardi (1996).

2. The division was not merely based on the nature of the work but the significant difference in income. In the 1970s, pattern making was the only occupation in garment factories that paid well enough to support a four-person family. The pattern maker's salary was ten times more than that of stitching assistants. See Eunseon Joo's (1999) work for more details.

3. A more literal translation would be "your body that knows how to work" (*ilhal jul aneun mom*).

4. All businesses are required to register with the district tax office. By law, South Korean citizens are required to participate in four insurance plans: the national pension program, national health insurance, unemployment insurance, and disaster insurance. All businesses with more than one full-time worker should cover a certain portion of their employees' insurance coverage. However, it is extremely rare that the garment workers have these forms of insurance as they are either self-employed as gaekgong or the home-

factory is not registered as a business. Among the home-factories in the Dongdaemun area, it is estimated that approximately 67.8 percent do not register as a business. Exact statistics are difficult to calculate because the home-factories are often hidden and refuse to register (MK Paesyeon saeop baljeon hyeophoe [MK Fashion Industry Development Association] 2008, 123–30).

5. According to Sylvia Yanagisako (2002), sentiments and commitments are involved in capital and kinship investments, and the practices cannot be reduced to "private strategies" and "practical self-interest" in opposition to the public and official male succession within the firm.

6. Such terms include *eonni*, for women up to their forties; *imo* (maternal aunt), for more mature women; and *ajeossi* or *samchon*, for most adult men.

7. Foundational works on the gendered division of labor from feminist perspectives have pointed out the limitations of separating domestic, reproductive activities from productive activities. See Olivia Harris and Kate Young (1981); and Karen Davies (1996).

8. J-K. Gibson-Graham (1996) criticized not only the way the early Marxist model neglected the complexities of production in the home sphere and women's labor, but she also critiqued the way feminist theorists do not challenge bounded spatial categories and imaginations, thus perpetuating the hierarchical order of the spaces of production.

9. Creed (2000) reviewed anthropological works on family forms and capitalist development and pointed out that new strategies of flexibility incorporated the efficiency of family economies.

10. See the work of Elisabeth Prügl and Irene Tinker (1997).

3. PASSIONATE IMITATION

1. Numerous intellectual property (IP) and labor disputes against fast-fashion mega brands took place frequently in the 2000s. The most notorious example would be Forever 21, a U.S-based company that was sued in 50 cases between 2001 and 2019 for IP infringement and labor law violations. See the overview in "The Many Lawsuits of Forever 21," *The Refinery Report,* October 2, 2014, https://www.thefineryreport.com/articles/2019/10/2/the-many-lawsuits-of-forever-21. Other incidents also drew media attention, including a factory worker's complaint message hidden in the garment tag found in a Zara store in Istanbul in 2017, and a fire in Dhaka's outsourcing factory for H&M. "Zara Clothes in Istanbul Tagged to Highlight Labor Dispute, " AP News, November 3, 2017, https://apnews.com/article/e41d4976b67f4616be772b118a9cb947; Kasperkevic, Jana, "Rana Plaza Bangladesh Collapse Fashion Working Conditions," The Guardian, May 31, 2016 (https://www.theguardian.com/business/2016/may/31/rana-plaza-bangladesh-collapse-fashion-working-conditions).

2. The office started in 2008 and reorganized to the current Ministry of Science, ICT and Future Planning.

3. The economic subject that these initiatives instituted signifies the advent of a new phase in Dongdaemun, one that is radically different from the former one comprising manufacturing laborers and traders and those whose creativity in producing "original designs" replaced the repetitive manual manufacturing, pirating, or mindless selling that had tarnished Dongdaemun's image in the past.

4. For well-known cases such as the domestic brands BangBang and Codes-Combine, see Jeonggeon Kim, "Dongdaemuni Mandŭlgo Segyega Imnŭnda," *Chosun Ilbo*, January 19, 2014, http://news.chosun.com/site/data/html_dir/2014/01/09/2014010900404.html?Dep0=twitter&d=2014010900404.

5. For this reason, it is not easy to pinpoint the "primary producer," and because of the informality of this market, where transactions are cash based, the receipt for tax reporting is many times retroactively made.

6. This scholarship claims that brand is a performance and analyzes the terms "counterfeit," "fake," or "copy" regarding their cultural contexts, moral assumptions, and semiotics (Narcassis 2012a ; Thomas 2016 ; Vann 2006).

7. The mobile phone is not only a medium of surveillance but also a measurement of their career. The numbers of factories, wholesale stores of textiles and garment materials, and other designers are what represent their professional ability and constitute the most important data. As they rarely use office, desk, and computer software, experienced designers sometimes wirelessly transmit data (such as contact information) to their junior coworkers through their cell phones.

8. MANI eventually managed to open its own workshop by working with emerging social entrepreneurs and drawing start-up funds from public investment agencies, such as the Ministry of Labor and the city of Seoul. However, this workshop and its own brand were discontinued after the initial three-year period. See chapter 4.

4. REDIRECTING THE FUTURE

1. The situation is similar to what Jennifer Chun (2011, 171–84) discussed about the dilemma of organizing workers in the context of prevailing irregular employment and independent contracts, on the one hand, and heightened antiunionism in South Korea and the United States.

2. The term *hai paesyeon* (high fashion) refers to upper-level brand-name clothes and is more expensive compared to mid- and low-brand clothes or *sijang ot* (marketplace clothes) or *bose ot* (nonbrand clothes).

3. Even as independent contractors, they often worked at stitching factories—see chapter 2.

4. I follow these activists, state entities, corporations, and individual workers as market actors, instead of divided from the major actors setting up the social project and its recipients or the social structure and the agent. Civil organizations, such as NGOs and nonprofit organizations (NPOs), which often represent the informal economy or civil society, function as agents of social experiments that further the market with different techniques for the creation and distribution of value (Elyachar 2005). Likewise, I intend to understand the market in plural forms (Gibson-Graham 1996; Miyazaki 2003) and see MANI's project of the alternative market as a node in different temporal and value networks.

5. For instance, see Um (2008).

6. This number accounts for the government certified social enterprises.

7. As of 2018, the number currently stood at 1,526 companies. See the Korea Social Enterprise Promotion Agency, accessed March 2, 2018, http://www.socialenterprise.or.kr/kosea/company.do.

8. With the success of venture capital companies, the Korean government inaugurated a venture enterprise certification program to stimulate the domestic economy during the 1997 Asian financial crisis. There were several venture capital competitions by the state and major corporations for small "venture enterprises." From the competition and certification, the small enterprises achieve a certified status that allowed low interest and tax, office space, and seed money for quick start-ups.

9. This is not new for "civic organizations" (*simindanche*) in Korea, which do not have clear divisions between the NGOs, NPOs, voluntary groups, or interest groups. Extensive research on the nature and function of civic organizations delineate the relationship between the state and civil society in the proliferation of those civic organizations during the late 1990s–2000s (He 2010; Koo 2002). Local scholarship also grew rapidly meanwhile, such as in the emergence of the NGO studies department in major universities and democracy studies, third-sector studies, and co-op studies in research institutes.

10. One such example was social campaigns of "re-reading Jeon's biography," which frequently took place in the 2000s. Often famous social activists came together and discussed the implications of this figure in their lives and in contemporary society. Numerous social theorists of South Korea comment that social activism in South Korea in the modernization period has been highly characterized by intellectuals' buchaeuisik (sense of indebtedness) toward labor. See, for instance, Korea Labor and Society Institute, "2010 nyeon Chun Taeil, keurigo nodong sahoe undong" [Year 2010, Chun Tail, and Labor and Social Movements], Korea Labor and Society Institute (website), May 3, 2013, http://www .klsi.org/content/2010. Noja Park (2016) furthers this discussion, contrasting this consciousness of indebtedness in the past with its disappearance in the present.

11. The term *buchae* connotes "liability" in the formal financial market and involves a broader sense of responsibilities than *bit* (debt).

12. The 386 Generation (*sampallyuk sedae*) is a term that refers to the generation of South Koreans born in the 1960s who were highly active politically as young adults and instrumental in the democracy movement of the 1980s. The term was coined in the early 1990s, hinting at the then latest computer model, the 386, and referring to people then in their thirties who attended university in the 1980s and had been born in the 1960s.

13. Joo-hwan Kim (2012) makes the further point that the recent tendency among Korean progressive camps in claiming corporate social responsibilities and ethical consumption as alternatives to neoliberalism will unintentionally result in the reinforcement of the neoliberalization of the government. According to him, this process makes a neoliberal mode of social responsibility: social actors, such as corporations, trade unions, NGOs, and consumers, begin to voluntarily undertake social responsibilities, instead of the state, which is not so much of social-moral solidarity but a neoliberal actor.

5. PACING THE FLOW

1. This "excess" and imbalance result from the contradictory desire of the state-led economy of the Philippines, which Tadiar (2004, 94) calls "the state bulimia."

2. Some of the vendors and manufacturers of metal tools and electronic appliances were relocated to a southeast part of Seoul, yet many of them were eventually displaced. While the metropolitan government of Seoul promised lots in newly developed commercial buildings, the sale or rent price tripled the estimate after the completion of construction. Even those who made it into the newly offered location by paying a higher price eventually suffered from the lack of outsourcing networks, which were integral for the type of production necessary for the small-scale manufacturing industry. See Kim and Kim (2015), who reviewed the process of displacement and conducted follow-up research on vendors who were relocated.

3. It is notable that Lee's office preferred the term "green growth" (*noksaek seongjang*) to the more common concept of "sustainable development" (*jisokkaneunghan baljeon*) and actively prioritized the Green Growth Committee as an independent constituency within the Ministry of Environment. After his term, the committee became part of the division of sustainable development. Some critiques compare these terms and claim that Lee's simplistic notion of "green growth" assumes a crude connection between the economy and the environment, excluding other components, such as society or community, that are supposed to be integral to sustainable development.

4. For instance, see Guy Solomon's (2010) thorough review.

5. For instance, *Lost Rivers*, a 2012 documentary film by Caroline Bacle, explores four international cities where people have taken care of their rivers and their efforts to excavate and restore subterranean rivers that have disappeared under urban landscape, including Cheonggyecheon in Seoul.

6. See the Seoul metropolitan government's report on telephone responses: "Simin 79.1%, Cheonggyecheon bokgwoneun Jalhanil" [79.1 percent of citizens responded "good job" to Cheonggyecheon restoration project], *Seoul Media Hub*, September 11, 2003, http://mediahub.seoul.go.kr/archives/139003.

7. To describe the strategy of this transition, the mayor coined a term "dijainomiksu" [designomix] combining design and economics. Oh, Sehun. Seoului Miraegyeongjaengnyeok [Seoul's Future Competiveness], Monthly Chosun Newsroom, January 10, 2010, http://monthly.chosun.com/client/news/viw.asp?ctcd=&nNewsNumb=201001100117.

8. Grounded in these campaigns and guidelines, Seoul was named "the World Design Capital" by the World Design Organization. Oh, Sehun. Seoului Miraegyeongjaengnyeok [Seoul's Future Competiveness], Monthly Chosun Newsroom, January 10, 2010, http://monthly.chosun.com/client/news/viw.asp?ctcd=&nNewsNumb=201001100117.

9. To pursue the DDP's harmony with the flow of the city, Hadid mentioned that she used a satellite image of the Han River. "Zaha Hadid on concepts and criticism," *Korea Joongang Daily*, July 1, 2009, http://mengnews.joins.com/view.aspx?aId=2906777.

10. This excavation affected the renaming of the nearby station: "Dongdaemun History and Cultural Museum Station," instead of the originally planned "Dongdaemun Design Plaza Station." For more details on the process and problems of the excavation, see A. Park (2011).

11. Zaha Hadid, "The Overflowing Energy of Dongdaemun Cannot Be Captivated in a Square Block," interview by Jinyoung Lee, *DongA Ilbo*, January 15, 2014, http://news.donga.com/more8/3/all/20140115/60170993/1#csidx8e512f3d23ffc3794bf0e460476b0bb.

12. The artwork was first exhibited in *There Is No Gold Medal in the Design Olympiad.*

13. Email interview with the artist, July 11, 2011.

14. Lee Eunhee, "Chuntaeildarieseo Saraoneun Areumdaun Cheongnyeonui Gieok" [The memory of beautiful young man reviving from Chun Taeil Bridge" *Minjuhwaundongginyeomsaeophoe* [Democracy foundation], November 16, 2010, http://www.kdemocracy.or.kr/blog/hopeplace/post/504; Beodeul Kim, "Urineun modu Chun Taeil ida" [We are all Chun Taeil], *Hakgyo Doseogwan Jeoneol* [School library journal], January 2, 2011, http://www.slj.co.kr/bbs/board.php?bo_table=book&wr_id=433&page=39.

15. The exceptions all signify objects and meanings relevant to the present day or future: Seungyo, named after the Seun building; Saebyeodari, named after the predawn market of Dongdaemun; Naraegyo, signifying the future of Dongdaemun as the hub of the global fashion industry; and Malgeundari, a Korean vernacular expression of Cheonggyecheon.

16. Street vendors were the first group driven out of the place and relocated to the Dongdaemun Baseball Stadium, which was eventually demolished for the construction of Dongdaemun Design Plaza, leading to their further eviction.

17. Jin Yoon, "Cheonggyecheoneseo doisarananeun chun taeil" (Chun Taeil revives in Cheonggyecheon), *Hangyeorye*, February 11, 2004, http://legacy.www.hani.co.kr/section-005000000/2004/02/005000000200402110313086.html.

18. Beodeul Kim, "Urineun modu chuntaeil-ida" [We are all Chun Taeil], *Hakgyo Doseogwan Jeoneol* [School library journal], January 2, 2011, http://www.slj.co.kr/bbs/board.php?bo_table=book&wr_id=433&page=39.

19. One of the famous examples would be the former president—then candidate—Park Geun-hye's visit to the bridge and attempt to offer a flower at the statue. In her election campaign, Park aggressively attempted an alleviation of the tension between the people and her father, the former military dictator Park Chung-hee, which Chun Taeil and his legacy vehemently protested. The Chun Taeil Foundation refused her visit due to her continuous neglect of labor strikes. Her planned contribution of a flower was also damaged.

20. For the spatial analysis of monuments, see Jung (2016). For an ethnographic account of cultural texts and narratives of former progressive activists, see Song (2009).

21. I am borrowing this phrase from Simpson's (2015, 439) analysis of a political rhetoric of liberal regime of settler colonialism.

22. Cho, "Cheonggyecheon Going Healthy—the Coming of Sweetfish," *Asia Gyeongje*, August 11, 2010, http://m.asiae.co.kr/view.htm?sec=n1&no=2010081108032281948#hi.

23. See the series of findings in the newspaper article Jong Yeong Nam, "Galgyeoni, euneo, geu daumen? Seoulsi cheonggyechon hongbo nunssal" [Dark chub, sweetfish, what's next? Seoul's Cheonggyecheon publicity campaign raises public's eyebrows], *Hangyoreh*, August 13, 2010, http://www.hani.co.kr/arti/society/environment/434809.html.

Bibliography

Abelmann, Nancy. 2003. *The Melodrama of Mobility: Women, Talk, and Class in Contemporary South Korea*. Honolulu: University of Hawaii Press.

Aitken, Stuart, and Matt Carroll. 1996. "Man's Place in the Home: Telecommuting, Identity and Urban Space." Paper presented at the Spatial Technologies, Geographic Information, and the City Research Conference by the National Center for Geographic Information and Analysis, Baltimore, MD, September 1996.

Allison, Anne. 1994. *Nightwork, Pleasure, and Corporate Masculinity in a Tokyo Hostess Club*. Chicago: University of Chicago Press.

Arvidsson, Adam, Giannino Malossi, and Serpica Naro. 2010. "Passionate Work? Labour Conditions in the Milan Fashion Industry." *Journal for Cultural Research* 14 (3): 295–309. https://doi.org/10.1080/14797581003791503.

Barraclough, Ruth. 2012. *Factory Girl Literature: Sexuality, Violence, and Representation in Industrializing Korea*. Berkeley: University of California Press.

Barry, Andrew, and Nigel Thrift. 2007. "Gabriel Tarde: Imitation, Invention and Economy." *Economy and Society* 36 (4): 509–25. https://doi.org/10.1080/03085140701589497.

Bear, Laura. 2014. "Doubt, Conflict, Mediation: The Anthropology of Modern Time." *Journal of the Royal Anthropological Institute* 20 (S1): 3–30. https://doi.org/10.1111/1467-9655.12091.

Bear, Laura, Karen Ho, Anna Tsing, and Sylvia Yanagisako. 2015. "Gens: A Feminist Manifesto for the Study of Capitalism." *Cultural Anthropology*, March 30: http://www.culanth.org/fieldsights/652-gens-a-feminist-manifesto-for-the-study-of-capitalism.

Bergeron, Suzanne. 2004. *Fragments of Development: Nation, Gender, and the Space of Modernity*. Ann Arbor: University of Michigan Press.

Berlant, Lauren Gail. 2011. *Cruel Optimism*. Durham, NC: Duke University Press.

Berndt, Christian, and Marc Boeckler. 2011. "Geographies of Markets: Materials, Morals and Monsters in Motion." *Progress in Human Geography* 35 (4): 559–67. https://doi.org/10.1177/0309132510384498.

Bestor, Theodore C. 2001. "Supply-Side Sushi: Commodity, Market, and the Global City." *American Anthropologist* 103 (1): 76–95. https://doi.org/10.1525/aa.2001.103.1.76.

———. 2004. *Tsukiji: The Fish Market at the Center of the World*. Berkeley: University of California Press.

Bianchini, Franco. 1995. "Night Cultures, Night Economies." *Planning Practice and Research* 10 (2): 121–26.

Bidet, Eric, and Hyung-Sik Eum. 2011. "Social Enterprise in South Korea: History and Diversity." *Social Enterprise Journal* 7 (1): 69–85. https://doi.org/10.1108/17508611111130167.

Bina, Olivia. 2013. "The Green Economy and Sustainable Development: An Uneasy Balance." *Environment and Planning C: Government and Policy* 31 (6): 1023–47. https://doi.org/10.1068/c1310j.

Bishop, Ryan, and Lillian S. Robinson. 1998. *Night Market: Sexual Cultures and the Thai Economic Miracle*. London: Routledge.

Bonacich, Edna. 1994. *Global Production: The Apparel Industry in the Pacific Rim*. Philadelphia: Temple University Press.

Borch, Christian. 2007. "Crowds and Economic Life: Bringing an Old Figure Back In." *Economy and Society* 36 (4): 549–73. https://doi.org/10.1080/03085140701589448.

Brennan, Teresa. 2004. *The Transmission of Affect*. Ithaca, NY: Cornell University Press.

Cairoli, M. Laetitia. 1998. "Factory as Home and Family: Female Workers in the Moroccan Garment Industry." *Human Organization* 57 (2): 181–89. https://doi.org/10 .17730/humo.57.2.082j824l32711736.

Cetina, Karin Knorr, and Urs Bruegger. 2000. "The Market as an Object of Attachment: Exploring Postsocial Relations in Financial Markets." *Canadian Journal of Sociology / Cahiers Canadiens de Sociologie* 25 (2): 141–68. https://dx.doi.org/10.2307/3341821.

Chang, Hsiao-hung. 2004. "Fake Logos, Fake Theory, Fake Globalization." *Inter-Asia Cultural Studies* 5 (2): 222–36. https://doi.org/10.1080/1464937042000236720.

Chang, Kyung-Sup. 1999. "Compressed Modernity and Its Discontents: South Korean Society in Transition." *Economy and Society* 28 (1): 30–55.

———. 2010. *South Korea under Compressed Modernity: Familial Political Economy in Transition*. New York: Routledge.

Chatterton, Paul, and Robert Hollands. 2003. *Urban Nightscapes: Youth Cultures, Pleasure Spaces and Corporate Power*. London: Routledge.

Cho, Haejoang. 1998. *Seongchaljeok Geundaeseonggwa Peminijeum* [Reflexive Modernity and Feminism]. Seoul: Ttohanaui Munhwa.

———. 2015. "The Spec Generation Who Can't Say 'No': Overeducated and Underemployed Youth in Contemporary South Korea." *positions* 23 (3): 437–62. https://www.muse .jhu.edu/article/593179.

Cho, Hee-Yeon. 2000. "Hanguk Enjioui Yeoksa: Hyeonhwanggwa Jeonmang" [The history of Korean NGOs: facts and prospect]. In *Enjioran Mueosinga* [What are NGOs], edited by Dongchun Kim, 127–56. Seoul: Areuke.

Cho, Mun Young, and Seung Chul Lee. 2017. "Sahoeui Wigiwa Sahoejeogingeosui Beomram" [The social crisis and the explosion of the social]. *Gyeongjewa Sahoe* [Economy and society] 113: 100–46. http://dx.doi.org/10.18207/criso.2017.113.100.

Cho, Myung-Rae. 2010. "The Politics of Urban Nature Restoration: The Case of Cheonggyecheon Restoration in Seoul, Korea." *International Development Planning Review* 32 (2): 145–65. https://doi.org/10.3828/idpr.2010.05.

Cho, Soon Kyoung. 1985. "The Labor Process and Capital Mobility: The Limits of the New International Division of Labor." *Politics and Society* 14 (2): 185–222.

Choi, Daebok. 2012. *Saebyeoge Moksumeul Geolda* [Betting my life on the dawn]. Seoul: Nexus Cross.

Choi, Jang-jip. 1989. *Labor and the Authoritarian State*. Honolulu: University of Hawaii Press.

Chu, Julie Y. 2014. "When Infrastructures Attack: The Workings of Disrepair in China." *American Ethnologist* 41 (2): 351–67. https://doi.org/10.1111/amet.12080.

Chu, Nellie. 2016. "The Emergence of 'Craft' and Migrant Entrepreneurship along the Global Commodity Chains for Fast Fashion in Southern China." *Journal of Modern Craft* 9 (2): 193–213. https://doi.org/10.1080/17496772.2016.1205278.

Chun, Jennifer Jihye. 2011. *Organizing at the Margins: The Symbolic Politics of Labor in South Korea and the United States*. Ithaca, NY: Cornell University Press.

Chun, Soonok. 2003. *They Are Not Machines: Korean Women Workers and Their Fight for Democratic Trade Unionism in the 1970s*. Cornwall, UK: Ashgate.

Chung, Jae A. 2003. "The Cultural Tempo of Korean Modernity: Celerity in Venture Industry." PhD diss., Rice University.

Clark, Hazel. 2008. "Slow + Fashion: An Oxymoron or a Promise for the Future." *Fashion Theory* 12 (4): 427–46. http://dx.doi.org/10.2752/175174108X346922.

Collins, Jane L. 2002. "Mapping a Global Labor Market Gender and Skill in the Globalizing Garment Industry." *Gender and Society* 16 (6): 921–40. http://doi.org/10.1177/089124302237895.

Constable, Nicole. 2009. "The Commodification of Intimacy: Marriage, Sex, and Reproductive Labor." *Annual Review of Anthropology* 38:49–64. http://doi.org/10.1146/annurev.anthro.37.081407.085133.

Crabbe, Jonathan Brian. 2014. "A Matter of Life and Death: A Durkheimian Analysis of South Korea's Suicide Epidemic." PhD diss., University of Sydney.

Crang, Mike. 2001. "Rhythms of the City: Temporalised Space and Motion." In *Timespace: Geographies of Temporality*, edited by Nigel Thrift and John May, 187–207. London: Routledge.

Crary, Jonathan. 2013. *24/7: Late Capitalism and the Ends of Sleep*. London: Verso.

Creed, Gerald W. 2000. "'Family Values' and Domestic Economies." *Annual Review of Anthropology* 29: 329–55. https://doi.org/10.1146/annurev.anthro.29.1.329.

Currid, Elizabeth. 2007. *The Warhol Economy: How Fashion, Art, and Music Drive New York City*. Princeton, NJ: Princeton University Press.

Davies, Karen. 1996. "Capturing Women's Lives: A Discussion of Time and Methodological Issues." *Women's Studies International Forum* 19 (6): 579–88.

Deeb, Lara. 2006. *An Enchanted Modern: Gender and Public Piety in Shi'i Lebanon*. Princeton, NJ: Princeton University Press.

Defourny, Jacques, Yu-Yuan Kuan, Eric Bidet, and Hyung-Sik Eum. 2011. "Social Enterprise in South Korea: History and Diversity." *Social Enterprise Journal* 7 (1): 69–85.

Denning, Michael. 2010. "Wageless Life." *New Left Review* 66:79–97.

Elyachar, Julia. 2005. *Markets of Dispossession: NGOs, Economic Development, and the State in Cairo*. Durham, NC: Duke University Press.

———. 2010. "Phatic Labor, Infrastructure, and the Question of Empowerment in Cairo." *American Ethnologist* 37 (3): 452–64.

Eun-Shil, Kim. 2000. "The Cultural Logic of the Korean Modernization Project and Its Gender Politics." *Asian Journal of Women's Studies* 6 (2): 50–77.

Evans, Graeme. 2009. "Creative Cities, Creative Spaces and Urban Policy." *Urban Studies* 46 (5–6): 1003–40.

Fabian, Johannes. 2014. *Time and the Other: How Anthropology Makes Its Object*. New York: Columbia University Press.

Folbre, Nancy. 2004. "A Theory of the Misallocation of Time." In *Family Time: The Social Organization of Care*, edited by Michael Bittman and Nancy Folbre, 7–24. London: Routledge.

Fraser, Nancy. 1989. *Unruly Practices: Power, Discourse, and Gender in Contemporary Social Theory*. Minneapolis: University of Minnesota Press.

Gandy, Matthew. 2014. *The Fabric of Space: Water, Modernity, and the Urban Imagination*. Cambridge: MIT Press.

———. 2017. "Urban Atmosphere." Critical Geographies 24 (3):353–374.

Garey, Anita Ilta. 1995. "Constructing Motherhood on the Night Shift: Working Mothers as Stay-at-Home Moms." *Qualitative Sociology* 18 (4): 415–37.

Ghertner, D. Asher. 2015. *Rule by Aesthetics: World-Class City Making in Delhi*. Oxford: Oxford University Press.

Gibson-Graham, J-K. 1996. *The End of Capitalism (as We Knew It): A Feminist Critique of Political Economy*. Minneapolis: University of Minnesota Press.

———. 2006. *A Postcapitalist Politics*. Minneapolis: University of Minnesota Press.

Green, Nancy L. 1996. "Women and Immigrants in the Sweatshop: Categories of Labor Segmentation Revisited." *Comparative Studies in Society and History* 38 (03): 411–33.

Gill, Rosalind, and Andy Pratt. 2008. "In the Social Factory? Immaterial Labour, Precariousness and Cultural Work." *Theory, Culture & Society* 25 (7–8): 1–30.

Hadfield, Phil. 2015. "The Night-Time City, Four Modes of Exclusion: Reflections on the Urban Studies Special Collection." *Urban Studies* 52 (3): 606–16. https://doi.org/10.1177/0042098014552934.

Hae, Laam. 2012. *The Gentrification of Nightlife and the Right to the City: Regulating Spaces of Social Dancing in New York.* London: Routledge.

Hanson, Susan, and Geraldine Pratt. 1995. *Gender, Work, and Space.* London: Routledge.

Harris, Olivia, and Kate Young. 1981. "Engendered Structures: Some Problems in the Analysis of Reproduction." In *The Anthropology of Pre-Capitalist Societies*, edited by Joel Kahn and Josep Llobera, 109–47. London: MacMillan Education.

Harvey, David. 1989. *The Condition of Postmodernity: An Enquiry into the Origins of Cultural Change.* Oxford: Wiley-Blackwell.

———. 2001. *Spaces of Capital: Toward a Critical Geography.* New York: Routledge.

Hassan, Robert. 2003. *The Chronoscopic Society: Globalization, Time, and Knowledge in the Network Economy.* New York: Peter Lang.

———. 2007. *24/7: Time and Temporality in the Network Society.* Stanford, CA: Stanford University Press.

Hatfield, DJ W. 2010. *Taiwanese Pilgrimage to China: Ritual, Complicity, Community.* New York: Palgrave Macmillan.

He, Lichao. 2010. "Social Movement Tradition and the Role of Civil Society in Japan and South Korea." *East Asia* 27 (3): 267–87. https://doi.org/10.1007/s12140-010-9113-0.

Heo, Eun Young. 2000. "Nodongsigan Danchukkwa Hyeonjangtujaeng" [Reduction of working hours and the struggles in the work site]. *Korean Institute of Labor Studies and Politics.* http://kilsp.jinbo.net/publish/2000/000707.htm

Hong, Seongtae. 2014. *Seouleui Gaehyeok* [The revolution of Seoul]. Gwacheon: Jininjin.

Hsieh, An-Tien, and Janet Chang. 2006. "Shopping and Tourist Night Markets in Taiwan." *Tourism Management* 27 (1): 138–45.

Joo, Eunseon. 1999. "Pyeonghwa Sijang Geuncheoui Uiryusaengsan Neteuwokeuwa Jiyeoknodongjaui Gyeonjesaenghwal Byeoncheon Gwanhan Yeongu" [Garment production network and local labor's economic life near Pyeonghwa Marketplace]. *Seoul Studies* 13:245–83.

Joy, Annamma, John F. Sherry Jr., Alladi Venkatesh, Jeff Wang, and Ricky Chan. 2012. "Fast Fashion, Sustainability, and the Ethical Appeal of Luxury Brands." *Fashion Theory* 16 (3): 273–95.

Jun, Jinsam. 2014. "Ddpe Sogabwa" [Be deceived by DDP]. *Hwanghae Munhwa* 83:425–32.

Jung, Ho-gi. 2016. "Siminsahoeui Sahoeundong Ginyeommul Geollipgwa Pyosang: '5·18'gwa '5wolundong'eul Jungsimeuro" [Construction and Representation of Memorial on the Social Movement by Civil Society: Focused on the May 18 Democratic Uprising and May-Movement]. *Geongjewa Sahoe* [Economy and Society] 94: 308–38. http://www.dbpia.co.kr/journal/articleDetail?nodeId=NODE01889512

Kal, Hong. 2011. "Flowing Back to the Future: The Cheongye Stream Restoration and the Remaking of Seoul." *Asia-Pacific Journal* 9 (21). https://apjjf.org/2011/9/27/Hong-KAL/3556/article.html.

Kang, Hyunsoo. 1995. "Yuyeonseong Ironui Bipanjeok Geomtowa Seoul Uiryu Sae-op Yuyeonhwae Gwanhan Yeongu" [Critical review of flexibility theory and the flexibilization of apparel industry in Seoul]. PhD diss., Seoul National University.

Kendall, Laurel. 2002. "Introduction." In *Under Construction: The Gendering of Modernity, Class, and Consumption in the Republic of Korea*, edited by Laurel Kendall, 1–24. Honolulu: University of Hawaii Press.

Kim, Gwangseok. 2015. *Ollain Syopingui Busanggwa Gyeongjejeok Hyogwa* [Emergence of online shopping and its economic impact]. Seoul: Hyundae Research Institute.

Kim, Hyun Mee. 2001. "Work, Nation and Hypermasculinity: The 'Woman' Question in the Economic Miracle and Crisis in South Korea." *Inter-Asia Cultural Studies* 2 (1): 53–68. https://doi.org/10.1080/14649370120039452.

Kim, Joo-hwan. 2012. "Sinjayujuui Sahoejeok Cheagimhwaui Gyebohak. [Genealogy of neoliberal social responsibilization]." *Gyeongjewa Sahoe* [Economy and society] 96: 210–51.

Kim, Ju Il, Chang Moo Lee, and Kun Hyuck Ahn. 2004. "Dongdaemun, a Traditional Marketplace Wearing a Modern Suit: The Importance of the Social Fabric in Physical Redevelopments." *Habitat International* 28 (1): 143–61. https://doi.org/10.1016/S0197-3975(03)00036-5.

Kim, Pan-Suk. 2002. "The Development of Korean NGOs and Governmental Assistance to NGOs." *Korea Journal* 42 (2): 279–303.

Kim, Seung-Kyung. 1997. *Class Struggle or Family Struggle? The Lives of Women Factory Workers in South Korea*. Cambridge: Cambridge University Press.

Kim, Won. 2005. *Yeogong 70: Geuneodeurui Banyeoksa* [Female Factory Workers 70: their anti-history]. Seoul: Imagine.

Kim, Won Bae. 1999. "Developmentalism and Beyond: Reflections on Korean Cities." *Korea Journal* 39 (3): 5–34.

Kim, Yanghee, and Yongnam Shin. 2000. *Jaeraesijangeseo Paesyeon Neteuwokeuro* [From traditional market to fashion network]. Seoul: SERI.

Kim, Yejin. 2008. *Babeun Gulmeodo Seutaireun Gulmjianneunda* [I may go foodless, but I never go styleless]. Seoul: Koloseum.

Kim, Kyeong-Min, and Yeon-soon Kim. 2015. "Dosijaesaengsaeobe Euihan Sanggwoneui Jaepongwa Hyanghu Gwaje" [A study of the reorganization of commercial areas and future challenges of urban regeneration: change of business activities and satisfaction levels of merchants and traders by the Cheonggyecheon Restoration Project]." *Jootaek Dosi Yeongu* [SH urban research and insight] 5 (1): 35–41.

Klein, Naomi. 2000. *No Logo*. Toronto: Vintage Canada.

Koo, Hagen. 2000. "The Dilemmas of Empowered Labor in Korea: Korean Workers in the Face of Global Capitalism." *Asian Survey* 40 (2): 227–50.

———. 2001. *Korean Workers: The Culture and Politics of Class Formation*. Ithaca, NY: Cornell University Press.

———. 2002. "Civil Society and Democracy in South Korea." *Good Society* 11 (2): 40–45.

Korean Apparel Industry Association. 2013. *Bongjeeopche Siltaejosa Kyeolgwabogoseo* [Reports on current stitching factories]. Seoul: Korean Apparel Industry Association.

Korea Labor Institute. 2012. *Seouljiyeok Bongje Uiryusaneob Iljari Changchuleul Wihan Goyong Seobiseu Gaeseon Bang-an* [Employment service enhancement for creating jobs in the garment industry in the Seoul metropolitan area]. Seoul: Ministry of Employment and Labor.

Krause, Elizabeth. *Tight Knit: Global Families and the Social Life of Fast Fashion*. Chicago: University of Chicago Press.

Kreitzman, Leon. 1999. *The 24-Hour Society*. London: Profile.

Ladner, Sam. 2009. "Agency Time: A Case Study of the Postindustrial Timescape and Its Impact on the Domestic Sphere." *Time and Society* 18 (2–3): 284–305.

Lamport, Mark A. 2018. *Encyclopedia of Christianity in the Global South*. London: Rowman & Littlefield.

Latour, Bruno, and Vincent Antonin Lépinay. 2009. *The Science of Passionate Interests: An Introduction to Gabriel Tarde's Economic Anthropology*. Chicago: Prickly Paradigm.

Leccardi, Carmen. 1996. "Rethinking Social Time: Feminist Perspectives." *Time and Society* 5 (2): 169–86.

Lee, Jo, and Tim Ingold. 2006. "Fieldwork on Foot: Perceiving, Routing, Socializing." In *Locating the Field: Space, Place and Context in Anthropology*, edited by Simon Coleman and Peter Collins, 67–86. Oxford: Berg.

Lee, Jong Hee, and Young Rong Lee. 2012. "24 Sigan Sahoeui Imyeon" [The other side of 24-hour society]. *Jinbopyeongron* [The radical review] 54:259–79.

Lee, Jong Youl, and Chad David Anderson. 2013. "The Restored Cheonggyecheon and the Quality of Life in Seoul." *Journal of Urban Technology* 20 (4): 3–22.

Lee, Myung-bak. 2007. *Cheonggyecheon Flows to Future*. Seoul: Random House.

Lee, Namhee. 2005. "Representing the Worker: The Worker-Intellectual Alliance of the 1980s in South Korea." *Journal of Asian Studies* 64 (4): 911–37.

———. 2007. *The Making of Minjung: Democracy and the Politics of Representation in South Korea*. Ithaca, NY: Cornell University Press.

Lee, Seung Hoon, and Ho Keun Song. 1994. "The Korean Garment Industry: From Authoritarian Patriarchism to Industrial Paternalism." In *Global Production: The Apparel Industry in the Pacific Rim*, edited by In Edna Bonacich, Lucie Cheng, Norma Chinchilla, Nora Hamilton, and Paul Ong, 147–161. Philadelphia: Temple University Press.

Lessinger, Johanna. 2002. "Work and Love: The Limits of Autonomy for Female Garment Workers in India." *Anthropology of Work Review* 23 (1–2): 13–18. http://doi.org/10.1525/awr.2002.23.1–2.13.

Listen to the City 2014. *Urban Drawings 3: Hidden History of Dongdaemun Design Park and the Star Architect*. Seoul: Listen to the City. http://www.listentothecity.org/filter/publication/Urban-Drawings-3-Hidden-History-of-Dongdaemun-Design-Park-and-the.

Lovatt, Andy, and Justin O'Connor. 1995. "Cities and the Night-Time Economy." *Planning Practice and Research* 10 (2): 127–34.

Manning, Paul. 2010. "The Semiotics of Brand." *Annual Review of Anthropology* 39:33–49. https://doi.org/10.2307/25735098.

Mariarinaldi, Bianca. 2007. "Landscapes of Metropolitan Hedonism the Cheonggyecheon Linear Park in Seoul." *Journal of Landscape Architecture* 2 (2): 60–73.

Martin-Jones, David. 2007. "Decompressing Modernity: South Korean Time Travel Narratives and the IMF Crisis." *Cinema Journal* 46 (4): 45–67.

Mathews, John A. 2012. "Green Growth Strategies: Korean Initiatives." *Futures* 44 (8): 761–69. https://doi.org/10.1016/j.futures.2012.06.002.

May, Jon, and Nigel Thrift. 2003. "Introduction." In *Timespace: Geographies of Temporality*, edited by Jon May and Nigel Thrift, 1–46. London: Routledge.

McIntyre, Magdalena. 2014. "Commodifying Passion." *Journal of Cultural Economy* 7 (1): 79–94. https://doi.org/10.1080/17530350.2013.851029.

McLuhan, Marshall, and H. Lapham Lewis. 1994. *Understanding Media: The Extensions of Man*. Cambridge, MA: MIT Press.

McRobbie, Angela. 2018. *Be Creative: Making a Living in the New Culture Industries*. Cambridge, MA: Polity Press.

Mills, Mary Beth. 2003. "Gender and Inequality in the Global Labor Force." *Annual Review of Anthropology* 32 (1): 41–62.

Mitter, Swasti, and Sheila Rowbotham. 2003. *Dignity and Daily Bread: New Forms of Economic Organization among Poor Women in the Third World and the First*. New York: Routledge.

Miyazaki, Hirokazu. 2003. "The Temporalities of the Market." *American Anthropologist* 105 (2): 255–65. https://www.jstor.org/stable/3567500.

MK Paesyeonsaeob Baljeon Hyeophoe [MK Fashion Industry Development Association]. 2008. *Dongademun Jiyeok Paesyeonsaneop mit Goyongsiltae Bunseoge Gwanhan Yeongu*. [A Study on the Fashion Industry and the Employment]. Seoul: Ministry of Labor.

Moon, Christina H. 2014. "The Secret World of Fast Fashion." *Pacific Standard*, March 17. https://psmag.com/the-secret-world-of-fast-fashion-9c899e0edb08#.57cx3uxgh.

Moore, Steven A., and Nathan Engstrom. 2004. "The Social Construction of 'Green Building' Codes." In *Sustainable Architectures: Critical Explorations of Green Building Practice in Europe and North America*, edited by Simon Guy and Steven Moore, 51–70. New York: Spon Press.

Munn, Nancy D. 1986. *The Fame of Gawa: A Symbolic Study of Value Transformation in a Massim (Papua New Guinea) Society*. Durham, NC: Duke University Press.

Nakassis, Constantine V. 2012a. "Counterfeiting What? Aesthetics of Brandedness and Brand in Tamil Nadu, India." *Anthropological Quarterly* 85 (3): 701–21. https://doi.org/10.1353/anq.2012.0046.

———. 2012b. "Brand, Citationality, Performativity." *American Anthropologist* 114 (4): 624–38. https://doi.org/10.1111/j.1548-1433.2012.01511.x.

———. 2016. *Doing Style: Youth and Mass Mediation in South India*. Chicago: University of Chicago Press.

Nelson, Laura C. 2000. *Measured Excess: Status, Gender, and Consumer Nationalism in South Korea*. New York: Columbia University Press.

Noritake, Ayami. 2009. "Gender, Aging and Agency: Street Entrepreneurs and Dressmakers in a Korean Marketplace." *Gender and Development* 17 (3): 403–15.

Odih, Pamela. 2003. "Gender, Work and Organization in the Time/Space Economy of 'Just-in-Time' Labour." *Time and Society* 12 (2–3): 293–314.

Ong, Aihwa. 2010. *Spirits of Resistance and Capitalist Discipline: Factory Women in Malaysia*. Albany: SUNY Press.

Osborne, Thomas. 2003. "Against 'Creativity': A Philistine Rant." *Economy and Society* 32 (4): 507–25. https://doi.org/10.1080/0308514032000141684.

Pang, Laikwan. 2008. "China Who Makes and Fakes: A Semiotics of the Counterfeit." *Theory, Culture and Society* 25 (7): 117–40. https://doi.org/10.1177/0263276408095547.

———. 2012. *Creativity and Its Discontents: China's Creative Industries and Intellectual Property Rights Offenses*. Durham, NC: Duke University Press.

Park, Aron. 2011. *Saebyeok Gido Iyagi* [Stories of predawn prayers]. Seoul: CLC.

Park, Chanho, and Gu-Jaecheon. 2010. *Saebyeok Gidohaneun CEO* [Dawn praying CEOs]. Seoul: Kanggateun Pyeonghwa.

Park, Noja. 2016. *Chusikhoesa Taehanminguk* [Korea, Inc.]. Seoul: Hangyeore.

Park, Seo Young. 2019a. "'My Skill': Attachments and Narratives of Garment Workers in South Korea." In *Gender and Class in Contemporary South Korea: Intersectionality and Transnationality*, edited by Hae Yeon Choo, John Lie, and Laura Nelson, 62–105. Berkeley: Institute of East Asian Studies at University of California, Berkeley.

———. 2019b. "Situating the Space of Labour: Activism, Work, and Urban Regeneration." In *On the Margins of Urban South Korea: Core Location as Method and Praxis*, edited by Jesook Song and Laam Hae, 163–85. Toronto: University of Toronto Press.

Parreñas, Rhacel Salazar, Hung Cam Thai, and Rachel Silvey. 2016. "Guest Editors' Introduction: Intimate Industries; Restructuring (Im)material Labor in Asia." *Positions* 24 (1): 1–15.

Patel, Reena. 2010. *Working the Night Shift: Women in India's Call Center Industry*. Stanford, CA: Stanford University Press.

Piore, Michael J., and Charles F. Sabel. 1984. *The Second Industrial Divide: Possibilities for Prosperity*. New York: Basic Books.

Prügl, Elisabeth, and Irene Tinker. 1997. "Microentrepreneurs and Homeworkers: Convergent Categories." *World Development* 25 (9): 1471–82. https://doi.org/10.1016 /S0305-750X(97)00043-0.

Raffles, Hugh. 2002. *In Amazonia: A Natural History*. Princeton, NJ: Princeton University Press.

Ren, Xuefei. 2008. "Architecture and Nation Building in the Age of Globalization: Construction of the National Stadium of Beijing for the 2008 Olympics." *Journal of Urban Affairs* 30 (2): 175–90. https://doi.org/10.1111/j.1467-9906.2008.00386.x.

Rhee, Jeongseok. "Saebyeok guidoui sinhakjeok banseong" [Theological reflections on predawn prayers]. *Ijeongseok gyosuui sinhak mundap* [Professor Rhee's Q&A in theology]. Accessed June 1, 2013. http://www.jsrhee.com/QA/prayer.htm.

Robinson, Michael Edson, and Gi-Wook Shin. 1999. *Colonial Modernity in Korea*. Cambridge, MA: Harvard University Asia Center.

Rofel, Lisa. 1999. *Other Modernities: Gendered Yearnings in China after Socialism*. Berkeley: University of California Press.

Roy, Ananya, and Aihwa Ong, eds. 2011. *World Cities: Asian Experiments and the Art of Being Global*. Malden, MA: Wiley-Blackwell.

Sassen, Saskia. 2000. "Spatialities and Temporalities of the Global: Elements for a Theorization." *Public Culture* 12 (1): 215–32.

———. 2003. "Analytic Borderlands: Economy and Culture in the Global City." In *A Companion to the City*, edited by Gale Bridge and Sophie Watson, 168–80. Oxford: Blackwell.

Seo, Dongjin. 2009. *Jayuui Uijii Jagi gyebarui Uiji* [The will to freedom and the will to self-development]. Paju: Dolbegae.

Seoul History Archives. 2011. *Changsin-Dong: Gonggangwa Ilsang* [Changsin-dong: space and the everyday life]. Seoul: Seoul History Archives.

Seoul Metropolitan Government. 2006. *Cheonggyecheon Bogwonsaeop Baekseo* [The Cheonggyecheon Restoration Project White Book]. Seoul: Seoul Metropolitan Government.

Sharma, Sarah. 2014. *In the Meantime: Temporality and Cultural Politics*. Durham, NC: Duke University Press.

Shaw, Robert. 2014. "Beyond Night-Time Economy: Affective Atmospheres of the Urban Night." *Geoforum* 51: 87–95.

Shin, Hyun Bang, and Soo Hyun Kim. 2016. "The Developmental State, Speculative Urbanization and the Politics of Displacement in Gentrifying Seoul." *Urban Studies* 53 (3): 540–59. http://doi-org.ccl.idm.oclc.org/10.1177/0042098014565745.

Simpson, Audra. 2015. "Whither Settler Colonialism." *Settler Colonial Studies* 6 (4): 438–45. https://doi.org/10.1080/2201473X.2015.1124427.

Smith, Richard G. 2003. "World City Topologies." *Progress in Human Geography* 27 (5): 561–82.

Solomon, Guy. "Asian Megacities, Free and Unfree: How Politics Has Shaped the Growth of Shanghai, Beijing, and Seoul." *City Journal: Past, Present, and Future of the City*, Autumn 2010. https://www.city-journal.org/html/asian-megacities-free-and-unfree -13332.html.

Song, Jesook. 2009. *South Koreans in the Debt Crisis: The Creation of a Neoliberal Welfare Society*. Durham, NC: Duke University Press.

———. 2014. *Living on Your Own: Single Women, Rental Housing, and Post-Revolutionary Affect in Contemporary South Korea*. Albany: SUNY Press.

Stewart, Kathleen. 2007. *Ordinary Affects*. Durham, NC: Duke University Press.

Tadiar, Neferti Xina M. 2004. *Fantasy Production: Sexual Economies and Other Philippine Consequences for the New World Order*. Hong Kong: Hong Kong University Press.

Thomas, Kedron. 2012. "Intellectual Property Law and the Ethics of Imitation in Guatemala." *Anthropological Quarterly* 85 (3): 785–815.

———. 2016. *Regulating Style: Intellectual Property Law and the Business of Fashion in Guatemala.* Berkeley: University of California Press.

Thompson, Edward P. 1967. "Time, Work-Discipline, and Industrial Capitalism." *Past and Present* 38:56–97.

Traweek, Sharon. 2009. *Beamtimes and Lifetimes: The World of High Energy Physicists.* Cambridge, MA: Harvard University Press.

Tsing, Anna. 2000. "The Global Situation." *Cultural Anthropology* 15 (3): 327–60. https://www.jstor.org/stable/656606.

———. 2009. "Supply Chains and the Human Condition." *Rethinking Marxism* 21 (2): 148–76. http://dx.doi.org/10.1080/08935690902743088.

Tu, Thuy Linh N. 2011. *The Beautiful Generation: Asian Americans and the Cultural Economy of Fashion.* Durham, NC: Duke University Press.

Um, Kiho. 2008. *Dakcheo, Segyehwa* [Shut up, globalization]. Seoul: Dangdae.

Vann, Elizabeth F. 2006. "The Limits of Authenticity in Vietnamese Consumer Markets." *American Anthropologist* 108 (2): 286–96.

Virilio, Paul, and Benjamin H. Bratton. 2006. *Speed and Politics: An Essay on Dromology.* New York: Semiotext(e).

Wajcman, Judy. 2014. *Pressed for Time: The Acceleration of Life in Digital Capitalism.* Chicago: University of Chicago Press.

Weeks, Kathi. 2011. *The Problem with Work: Feminism, Marxism, Antiwork Politics, and Postwork Imaginaries.* Durham, NC: Duke University Press.

Wilson, Ara. 2004. *The Intimate Economies of Bangkok: Tomboys, Tycoons, and Avon Ladies in the Global City.* Berkeley: University of California Press.

———. 2012. "Anthropology and the Radical Philosophy of Antonio Negri and Michael Hardt." *Focaal—Journal of Global and Historical Anthropology* 64:3–15. https://doi.org/10.3167/fcl.2012.640101.

Woo, Seokhoon. 2008. *Jikseondeureui Daehanminguk* [South Korea of straight lines]. Seoul: Woongjin.

Yanagisako, Sylvia Junko. 2002. *Producing Culture and Capital: Family Firms in Italy.* Princeton, NJ: Princeton University Press.

———. 2012. "Immaterial and Industrial Labor: On False Binaries in Hardt and Negri's Trilogy." *Focaal—Journal of Global and Historical Anthropology* 64:16–23.

Yanagisako, Sylvia, and Lisa Rofel. 2019. *Fabricating Transnational Capitalism: A Collaborative Ethnography of Italian-Chinese Global Fashion.* Durham, NC: Duke University Press.

Yoon, Hee Seok. "Ollain syopingmol, changeop pummogi bakkuinda." [The start-up items of online shopping malls are changing]. 2013. *ETNEWS,* May 7, 2013, http://www.etnews.com/201305070366.

Yoon, Jungrok. 2009. *Homo Dijikuseuro Jinhwahara* [Evolve to *Homo digicus*]. Seoul: Saengagui Namu.

Yum, Bokkyu. 2015. "Cheonggyecheon Bokkuwa 1960nyeondaejeok Gongganeui Tansaeng" [Covering Cheonggyecheon stream and the birth of a 1960s space]. *Yeoksabipyeongsa* [Critical review history] 113:119–40.

Zaloom, Caitlin. 2006. *Out of the Pits: Traders and Technology from Chicago to London.* Chicago: University of Chicago Press.

Zelizer, Viviana. 2005. *The Purchase of Intimacy.* Princeton, NJ: Princeton University Press.

Index

NOTE: Page numbers in *italics* denote illustrations.

CPSIA information can be obtained
at www.ICGtesting.com
Printed in the USA
LVHW091912060521
686706LV00006B/359